PRAIRIE GRASSES
Identified and Described
by Vegetative Characters

KEITH F. BEST
JAN LOOMAN
and
J. BADEN CAMPBELL

Research Station
Swift Current
Saskatchewan

Publication 1413   1971
CANADA DEPARTMENT OF AGRICULTURE

© Minister of Supply and Services Canada 1977

Available by mail from

Printing and Publishing
Supply and Services Canada
Ottawa, Canada, K1A 0S9

or through your bookseller.

Catalogue No. A53-1413   Canada: $4.50
                                Other countries: $5.40

Price subject to change without notice.
1st printing 1971
Reprinted 1974
Reprinted 1976
Reprinted 1977

TRI-GRAPHIC PRINTING (OTTAWA) LTD.
CONTRACT NO.: 65826-01688

CONTENTS

A rule in centimeters and inches is located on the inside of the
back cover.

Foreword

Most of the 104 grasses described and illustrated in this book are native species that grow on the rangelands of the Prairie Provinces of Canada. Several have been introduced from other countries and they are grown for hay and pasture on cultivated land. A few are persistent weeds in grainfields and pastures. Some are abundant throughout the prairie region; others grow only in narrowly defined habitats. Many are valuable forage species in southern British Columbia, Eastern Canada, and Northern United States, as well as in the Prairie Provinces.

This book is a revision of Technical Bulletin No. 50, by S. E. Clarke, J. A. Campbell, and W. Shevkenek, published in 1944 and reprinted as Publication No. 762 in 1950. It was entitled *The Identification of Certain Native and Naturalized Grasses by their Vegetative Characters.* In the present revision diagrammatic drawings have been added and the key has been simplified. All descriptions have been rewritten. The present authors acknowledge the contributions taken from the original publication. They are also grateful for use made of *The Identification of Certain Native and Naturalized Hay and Pasture Grasses by their Vegetative Characters,* by F. S. Nowosad, D. E. Newton Swales, and W. G. Dore, Macdonald College Technical Bulletin No. 16, 1946.

It is often necessary to identify a grass before it has flowered, after flowers are no longer present, or, indeed, even after some of the plant has been eaten by animals. Such a need is met by this publication. It provides a key that makes use of vegetative characters only. These characters are present in the roots, stalks, and leaves of grasses.

THE GRASS PLANT

It is strange that grass, the most common plant in most places in the world, is intimately known to rather few people. The structure of a grass is, however, just as easy to understand as that of any other plant. A typical grass is shown in Figure 1.

The *roots* of grasses, like those of other land plants, serve to anchor the plant in the soil and to conduct water and nutrients in solution from the soil to the plant parts. The main body of a grass comprises the *culm,* or stalk, and the *leaves.* In most grasses the culm is hollow and is composed of several tubes closed at the joints by solid tissue. The joints are *nodes;* the portions between them are *internodes.* One or more buds, which are undeveloped leaf or flower branches, may form at every node.

The leaves are arranged in two ranks, that is, alternately on opposite "sides" of the culm. The base of each leaf is at a node. The expanded upper part of the leaf is the *blade;* the lower part, which is usually split on the "side" opposite the blade, surrounds the culm, and is called the *sheath.*

At the junction of the sheath and blade, and facing the culm, there is almost always a small appendage termed the *ligule.* At the same place, but on the outer or lower "side," there is a band called the *collar.* Usually, on either side of the split in the sheath the collar bears projections termed *auricles.*

An important feature in the identification of grasses is the *emerging leaf,* that is, the new growth as it emerges from the sheath. The emerging leaf is described on page 13.

A description of the flowers is not needed here, because in this book grasses are identified by vegetative characters alone.

A fuller account of essential vegetative characters follows.

VEGETATIVE PARTS

Roots

In grasses there are mainly three types of roots (Figure 2). A fibrous root branches in all downward directions from the crown, as in crested wheat grass (*Agropyron cristatum*) or rough fescue (*Festuca scabrella*). Rhizomatous roots, or rootstalks, are actually underground stems from which stalks and roots develop at intervals, as in western wheat grass (*Agropyron smithii*), smooth brome (*Bromus inermis*), and some other grasses. Stolons are horizontal stalks that root at the nodes. The roots of creeping bent (*Agrostis palustris*) are stoloniferous.

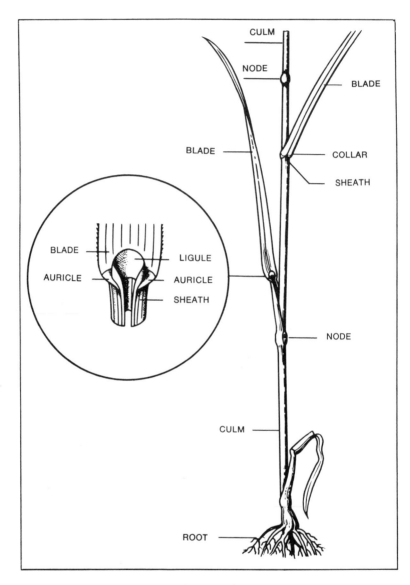

Figure 1   A grass plant, showing the vegetative parts.

Blade

The blade (Figure 3) is usually long and narrow. Though ordinarily rather flat, it may be V-shaped, folded, or rounded. When it is so tightly folded that it seems to be solid and cylindrical, it is termed bristle-like. A rounded leaf may be U-shaped, cylindrical with one margin overlapping the other (convolute), or cylindrical with margins turned inward toward the midrib (involute). A blade may be constricted at the base, or sometimes twisted. Its tip may be sharp-pointed or boat-shaped, and the general shape may be tapered or mostly with parallel sides (Figure 4). The surface may be smooth, rough, or hairy, and the margins smooth, without hairs (glabrous), or with a fringe of hairs (ciliate). Veins may be so prominent on the upper surface that they form ridges. On the lower surface the midvein or midrib may be prominent enough to form a keel.

Figure 2   Types of grass roots.

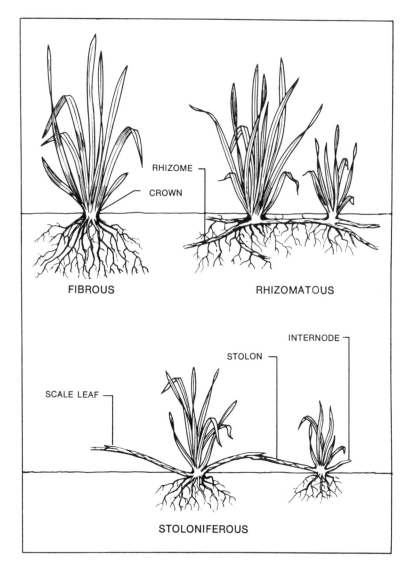

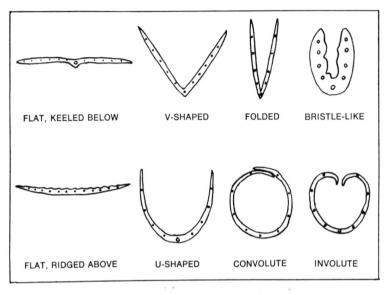

FLAT, KEELED BELOW   V-SHAPED   FOLDED   BRISTLE-LIKE

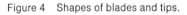

FLAT, RIDGED ABOVE   U-SHAPED   CONVOLUTE   INVOLUTE

Figure 3   Shapes of blades, in cross section.

Figure 4   Shapes of blades and tips.

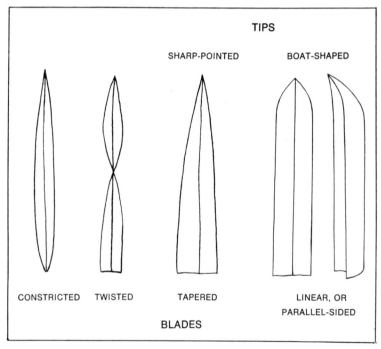

TIPS

SHARP-POINTED   BOAT-SHAPED

CONSTRICTED   TWISTED   TAPERED   LINEAR, OR
                                                                        PARALLEL-SIDED

BLADES

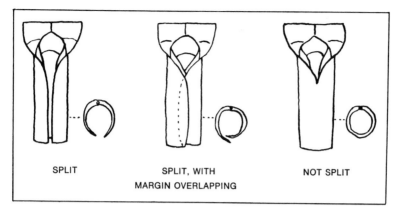

SPLIT   SPLIT, WITH   NOT SPLIT
MARGIN OVERLAPPING

Figure 5   Split and unsplit sheaths, viewed directly and in cross section.

Figure 6   Ligules, showing *(upper row)* types (and, *right,* a leaf without a ligule), *(middle row)* shapes, and *(lower row)* margins.

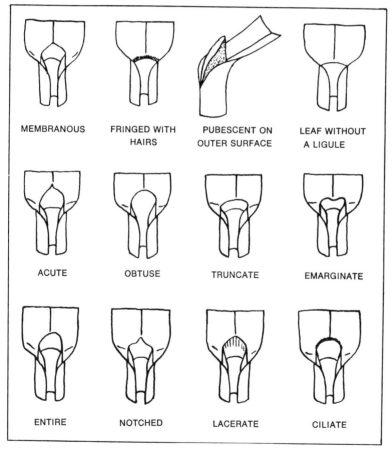

MEMBRANOUS   FRINGED WITH   PUBESCENT ON   LEAF WITHOUT
               HAIRS   OUTER SURFACE   A LIGULE

ACUTE   OBTUSE   TRUNCATE   EMARGINATE

ENTIRE   NOTCHED   LACERATE   CILIATE

Sheath

The sheath may be round or compressed. Occasionally it is keeled at the midrib. It is usually of a paler shade of green than the blade, and is often tinged with pink or purple at its base. These tints are not consistent enough to be of much value in identification, except in a few grasses such as meadow foxtail (*Alopecurus pratensis*). A sheath may be split completely, split with one margin overlapping the other, or without a split (Figure 5). A ruptured sheath must be distinguished from one that is naturally split.

Ligule

The ligule may be a membrane or a fringe of hairs. In some species the ligule is not present. In texture and color it varies from thin and white, as in Canby blue grass (*Poa canbyi*), to thick and opaque, as in fringed brome (*Bromus ciliatus*). The length of a ligule may vary within a species, but its shape and color and the character of its margins are usually quite constant. The outer surface of the ligule is usually smooth, but it may be pubescent, as in reed canary grass (*Phalaris arundinacea*) and some species of *Agrostis*. The types, shapes, and margins of ligules are shown in Figure 6. Large ligules and those in old or dry material may be so frayed and broken that they are useless for identification purposes.

Figure 7   Types of collars.

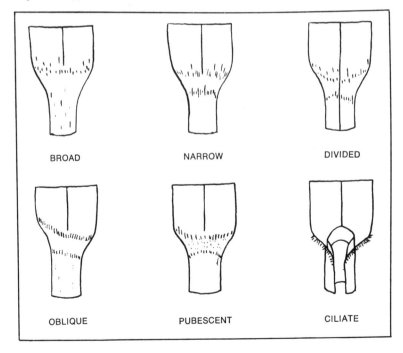

BROAD   NARROW   DIVIDED

OBLIQUE   PUBESCENT   CILIATE

Collar

The band that forms the collar (Figure 7) may be vertically broad or narrow, continuous, or divided by a midrib. If it extends diagonally it is called oblique. The collar is usually smooth, but it may be hairy (pubescent) over the whole surface, as in quack grass (*Agropyron repens*), or it may have minute hairs (cilia) on the inner and lowermost portion of the margin. It is usually pale green or yellowish green, but it may be temporarily tinged with red, as in yellow foxtail (*Setaria glauca*).

Figure 8　Shapes of auricles and *(right)* a collar without auricles.

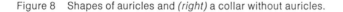

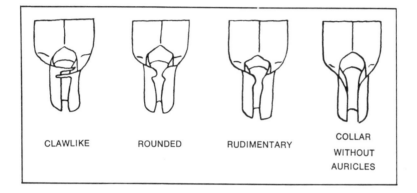

| CLAWLIKE | ROUNDED | RUDIMENTARY | COLLAR WITHOUT AURICLES |

Auricles

Auricles (Figure 8) are appendages extending from the collar. They may be horizontally clawed, fully or slightly rounded, or rudimentary. Sometimes they are not present. When old or dry specimens are being examined care must be taken to avoid breaking off the auricles.

Emerging Leaf

A developing leaf is closely surrounded by the sheath of the previously developed leaf (Figure 9). In the developing state, a blade may be con-duplicate, that is, folded at the midvein with the margins meeting, or it may be rolled lengthwise with either one margin overlapping the other (convolute) or both margins turned inward toward the midrib (involute). Conduplicate leaves usually form a laterally compressed shoot, rolled leaves usually a cylindrical one. There are exceptions. In yellow foxtail (*Setaria glauca*) and barnyard grass (*Echinochloa crusgalli*) the leaves are rolled in flattened shoots, whereas in poverty oat grass (*Danthonia spicata*), June grass (*Koeleria cristata*), and certain fescues, the folded leaves are in round shoots. In plains reed grass (*Calamagrostis montanensis*) and Nuttall's alkali grass (*Puccinellia nuttalliana*) the leaves are involute in somewhat rounded shoots.

The shape of the emerging leaves can best be seen when the stalk is cut just below the ligule and examined with a hand lens.

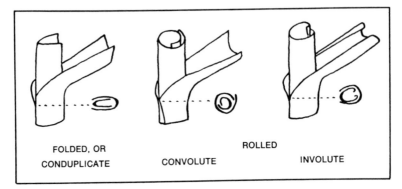

FOLDED, OR CONDUPLICATE   CONVOLUTE   ROLLED   INVOLUTE

Figure 9 Shapes of emerging leaves, with, at right of each leaf, a cross-section view at the juncture of leaf blade and sheath.

OTHER GRASSLIKE PLANTS

Some common plants, mainly the sedges and rushes, are in certain ways similar to grasses. Table 1 presents comparative information.

TABLE 1   A COMPARISON OF PLANT PARTS IN THE GRASSES, SEDGES, AND RUSHES

Character	Gramineae (grasses)	Cyperaceae (sedges)	Juncaceae (rushes)
Culm	Usually hollow; cylindrical or flattened Nodes conspicuous	Filled with pith, rarely hollow, usually three-sided Nodes indistinct	Filled with spongelike pith, cylindrical Nodes indistinct
Leaf arrangement	Two-ranked	Three-ranked	Three-ranked
Leaf blade	Usually flat; often folded, involute, or bristle-like; glabrous or pubescent	Flat, folded, or bristle-like; rarely pubescent	Channeled or round, usually glabrous
Leaf margins	Smooth, scabrous, or ciliate	Usually scabrous	Smooth
Leaf sheath	Usually split, occasionally closed	Usually closed	Open or closed
Ligule	Usually present	Absent or weakly developed	Absent or weakly developed
Collar	Distinct	Indistinct	Indistinct
Auricles	Present or absent	Absent	Absent

BIBLIOGRAPHY

Budd, A. C., and K. F. Best. 1964. Wild plants of the Canadian Prairies. Publication 983. Research Branch, Canada Department of Agriculture, Ottawa. 519 p.

Campbell, J. B., K. F. Best, and A. C. Budd. 1969. Ninety-nine range forage plants of the Canadian Prairies. Publication 964. Canada Department of Agriculture, Ottawa. 102 p.

Chase, Agnes. 1959. First book of grasses. Smithsonian Institution, Washington, D.C. 127 p.

Hitchcock, A. S. 1951. Manual of the grasses of the United States. Second edition, revised by Agnes Chase. United States Department of Agriculture Miscellaneous Publication No. 200. United States Government Printing Office, Washington, D.C. 1051 p.

Hubbard, W. A. 1955. The grasses of British Columbia. British Columbia Provincial Museum, Department of Education Handbook No. 9, Victoria, B.C. 204 p.

Moss, E. H. 1959. Flora of Alberta. University of Toronto Press, Toronto. 546 p.

Nowosad, F. S., D. E. Newton Swales, and W. G. Dore. 1946. The identification of certain native and naturalized hay and pasture grasses by their vegetative characteristics. Macdonald College Technical Bulletin No. 16. Macdonald College, Que. 78 p.

Scoggan, H. J. 1957. Flora of Manitoba. National Museum of Canada Bulletin No. 140, Biological Series No. 47. Canada Department of Northern Affairs and National Resources, Ottawa. 619 p.

United States Forest Service. 1937. Range plant handbook. Prepared by Forest Service, United States Department of Agriculture. Government Printing Office, Washington, D.C. 842 p.

GLOSSARY

Definitions are limited to the sense of the word as it applies to vegetative parts of grasses in this publication.

acuminate	*of a blade, ligule, stolon, or rhizome:* gradually tapering to a sharp point
acute	*of a blade or ligule:* abruptly sharp-pointed
annual	*of a plant:* (noun) a plant that completes its life cycle in one growing season (adjective) completing the life cycle in one growing season
ascending	*of a plant part:* sloping upward
auricle	an appendage of a collar
blade	the portion of the leaf above the sheath
bulbous	*of a stalk:* having a bulb-like base
chartaceous	*of a ligule:* having the texture of writing paper
ciliate	*of a blade, collar, or ligule:* fringed with fine hairs
ciliolate	*of a ligule or blade margin:* fringed with minute hairs
clasping	*of an auricle:* having the appendage extending directly into the collar and partly or completely surrounding the blade
collar	the band on the outer or lower "side" of the leaf at the junction of the sheath and the blade

compressed	*of a sheath:* flattened laterally
conduplicate	*of a leaf:* folded together lengthwise in the emerging leaf
constricted	*of a collar:* narrowed at the midpoint
continuous	*of a collar:* extending from one margin of the sheath to the other
convolute	*of a leaf:* rolled lengthwise in the emerging leaf, with one margin overlapping the other
coriaceous	*of a leaf:* leathery in texture
corrugated	*of a ligule:* having alternating ridges and grooves
crown	*of a plant:* the region from which both stalks and roots grow
decumbent	*of a stalk:* curved upward from a horizontal or slightly inclined base
divided	*of a collar:* separated at the midrib
emarginate	*of a ligule:* notched at the tip
entire	*of a blade or ligule:* having the margins continuous and not in any way divided
fascicle	*of leaves:* a compact cluster
fibrillose	*of a root:* having fine fibers
filiform	*of a blade:* very slender; threadlike
flaccid	*of a blade:* lax and weak; lacking rigidity
flexuous	*of a blade:* having alternate opposite curvatures
glabrous	*of a blade, collar, or sheath:* without hairs
glaucous	*of a blade:* covered with a waxy layer, which gives the plant part a bluish green color
hirsute	*of a blade or sheath:* having coarse, straight, rather stiff hairs
hispid	*of a blade or sheath:* having stiff hairs or bristles
hyaline	*of a sheath margin:* thin and translucent or transparent
hybrid	*of a plant:* a cross between two species of plants
involute	*of a blade or an emerging leaf:* having margins rolled over the upper surface toward the midrib
keel	a ridge on the back of a sheath or blade usually along the midrib
lacerate	*of a ligule:* having margins deeply and irregularly cut
ligule	a thin appendage projecting from the inner surface of a leaf at the junction of the sheath and blade
linear	*of a blade:* long and narrow with parallel sides
membranous	*of a ligule:* thin, rather soft, and more or less translucent and pliable
midrib	*of a blade:* the central vein
muriform	*of cells:* arranged like rows of bricks

oblique	*of a collar:* slanting and of varying width
obtuse	*of a ligule:* blunt or rounded at the tip
papillose	*of a blade or sheath:* having minute nipple-shaped projections
perennial	*of a plant:* (noun) a plant that lives for more than two years (adjective) living more than two years
pilose	*of a plant part:* having soft, fairly long, straight hairs
procumbent	*of a stalk:* partly prostrate
prostrate	*of a stalk:* trailing along the ground
puberulent	*of a sheath:* having fine minute hairs
pubescent	*of a plant part:* having soft fine hairs
retrorse	*of hairs:* bent downward or backward
rhizome	an underground stalk from which, at intervals, shoots arise above and roots descend below; also called root-stalk
ridged	*of a blade:* having raised veins
rootstalk	a rhizome
rudimentary	*of a plant part:* imperfectly developed
scaberulous	*of a blade:* having minute protuberances that are rough to the touch
scabrous	*of a blade:* having small protuberances that are rough to the touch
scarious	*of a sheath or blade:* having rather thin, translucent, not green, dry margins
serrate	*of a ligule or blade margin:* having sharp teeth
serrulate	*of a ligule:* having fine teeth
sheath	the lower part of the leaf that surrounds the stem or shoot
stolon	an aboveground creeping stem that roots at the nodes
stoloniferous	*of a plant:* bearing stolons
stoma	(plural: stomata) a minute opening in the surface of a leaf
striate	*of a sheath:* having very narrow longitudinal lines of darker or lighter color than the adjacent tissue
truncate	*of a ligule:* having the tip seemingly cut off at a right angle to the midrib
tufted	*of plants:* having shoots in a loose, compact, or dense cluster arising from a crown
undulate	*of a ligule:* having a wavy summit
vein	*of a blade or sheath:* one of the parallel structures that serve to support the leaf
villose	*of a plant part:* having long, soft hairs

THE IDENTIFICATION AND DESCRIPTION OF GRASSES

HOW TO IDENTIFY A GRASS

The following key contains a series of two or more contrasting statements. Compare the characteristics of the grass you want to identify with the distinguishing feature(s) mentioned in the statements. If the character(s) are present in your grass, and the statement does not lead directly to a species name, notice the number at the extreme *right* of the statement. Go to this number at the *left* of the page and read the adjoining statement(s). Follow this procedure until you read a statement that is followed by a botanical name. This is the name of the grass you have been trying to identify.

In using the key you may need to refer to the glossary, which immediately precedes this section. Note also that for the purpose of this key and in the descriptions of species the word *blades* implies and refers only to mature blades near the collar. To distinguish some characters you may need to use a ten-power hand lens. Individual characters may show some variation. Such variability, as well as changes brought about by shrinkage or distortion in dried or old material, should be taken into account when you use the key.

VEGETATIVE-CHARACTER KEY

1 Auricles present 2
  Auricles absent or rudimentary 14
2 Plants with rhizomes 3
  Plants without rhizomes 7
3 Rhizomes long, white; blades stiff, glaucous;
    collar and auricles usually purplish .... *Agropyron smithii*
  Rhizomes long, yellowish white; blades not
    stiff, with lines of stomata on lower surface .. *Agropyron repens*
  Rhizomes and blades not as above 4
4 Blades less than 10 mm wide 5
  Blades more than 10 mm wide 6
5 Rhizomes numerous; blades to 6 mm wide, flat
    or involute, stiff, dull green .... *Agropyron dasystachyum*
  Rhizomes few; blades to 8 mm wide, flat, lax,
    glossy green beneath; ligule entire .... *Festuca elatior*
  Rhizomes few; blades to 10 mm wide, pale
    green; ligule serrate .... *Agropyron intermedium*

19

6 Rhizomes short; often absent in old plants;
    ligule truncate; collar broad, continuous ... *Elymus canadensis*
  Rhizomes slender and scaly; ligule truncate;
    collar narow, indistinct, divided .... *Elymus innovatus*
  Rhizomes short, thick; ligule obtuse,
    lacerate; collar narrow .... *Elymus condensatus*
7 Blades more than 10 mm wide 8
  Blades less than 10 mm wide 9
8 Sheath with hyaline margins; collar broad;
    ligule very short, about 0.5 mm; blades green .. *Elymus virginicus*
  Sheath with scarious margins; collar broad;
    ligule to 2 mm; blades green .... *Elymus canadensis*
  Sheath with scarious margins; collar narrow;
    ligule to 2 mm; blades glaucous .... *Elymus glaucus*
9 Plants annual; blades acuminate, twisted,
    bluish green .... *Lolium persicum*
  Plants perennial; blades not twisted 10
10 Blades soft pubescent on upper surface ..... *Agropyron cristatum*
  Blades not pubescent 11
11 Sheath usually compressed, reddish at base;
    blades acuminate, glossy beneath .... *Lolium perenne*
  Sheath not compressed, margins hyaline 12
  Sheath not compressed, margins scarious 13
12 Collar broad, continuous; blades prominently
    veined; no lines of stomata on lower surface;
    ligule truncate .... *Elymus junceus*
  Collar broad, continuous, constricted at midrib;
    blades strongly veined, firm, rigid, with lines
    of stomata on lower surface; ligule acute ..... *Elymus angustus*
  Collar distinct, continuous; blades firm, midrib
    prominent near collar; ligule serrate,
    very short .... *Agropyron elongatum*
  Collar indistinct; blades not prominently
    veined; ligule truncate .... *Agrohordeum macounii*
13 Plants densely tufted; collar continuous;
    midrib prominent on lower surface of blade;
    sheath glabrous .... *Agropyron spicatum*
  Plants loosely tufted; collar divided;
    midrib not prominent on lower surface of
    blade; sheath pubescent .... *Agropyron subsecundum*
14 Plants with rhizomes 15
  Plants without rhizomes; roots fibrous 45
15 Tips of blades boat-shaped 16
  Tips of blades acute or acuminate 19
16 Ligule to 5 mm long, white, acuminate; sheath with crossveins 17
  Ligule to 3 mm long, greenish, truncate to acute; sheath
    without crossveins 18
17 Blades narrow, to 6 mm wide; sheath tinged
    with purple; blades not conspicuously
    crossveined .... *Glyceria striata*
  Blades broad, to 15 mm wide; sheath pale green;
    blades conspicuously crossveined .... *Glyceria grandis*

18 Sheath strongly flattened, sharply keeled;
    collar divided; blades bluish green . . . . *Poa compressa*
   Sheath not strongly flattened or keeled;
    collar continuous; blades glossy dark green . . . . . . *Poa pratensis*
   Sheath not strongly flattened or keeled;
    collar usually continuous; blades bluish green . . . *Poa glaucifolia*
19 Blades more than 10 mm wide 20
   Blades less than 10 mm wide 25
20 Sheath closed to near the top 21
   Sheath split 22
21 Midrib of blade extending partway down sheath;
    blade and sheath often pubescent; sheath
    purplish at base . . . . *Bromus pumpellianus*
   Midrib of blade not extending down sheath;
    blade and sheath glabrous; sheath not
    purplish at base . . . . *Bromus inermis*
22 Plants of dry habitats 23
   Plants of wet habitats 24
23 Sheath margins hyaline; sheath usually somewhat pubescent
    above, light green . . . . *Calamovilfa longifolia*
   Sheath margins scarious and villose; sheath
    glabrous, strongly veined . . . . *Panicum virgatum*
24 Ligule membranous, to 5 mm long, white,
    acute or obtuse; blades to 15 mm wide . . . . *Phalaris arundinacea*
   Ligule a fringe of hairs; blades to 15 mm
    wide, distinctly veined, smooth
    and shiny below . . . . *Spartina pectinata*
   Ligule a fringe of hairs; blades to 30 mm
    wide, not distinctly veined, dull below . . *Phragmites communis*
25 Rhizomes very short or absent 26
   Rhizomes elongated 33
26 Emerging leaves folded 27
   Emerging leaves rolled 28
27 Blade strongly veined; ligule very short;
    collar indistinct; plants loosely tufted . . . . *Festuca rubra*
   Blade strongly veined; ligule very short;
    collar indistinct; plants densely tufted . . . . *Festuca scabrella*
   Blade not strongly veined; ligule to 2 mm
    long; collar broad, continuous . . . . *Andropogon scoparius*
28 Ligule a fringe of hairs 29
   Ligule membranous 30
29 Blades to 7 mm wide, twisted;
    sheath usually pubescent . . . . *Bouteloua curtipendula*
   Blades to 3 mm wide, usually strongly
    curled; sheath glabrous or somewhat pilose . . . *Bouteloua gracilis*
30 Sheath compressed or flattened, pubescent or
    scabrous 31
   Sheath round, glabrous 32
31 Plants densely tufted, blades to 3 mm wide;
    ligule very short, ciliate . . . . *Sporobolus heterolepis*
   Plants not densely tufted; blades to 10 mm
    wide; ligule to 3 mm long, ciliate or
    lacerate . . . . *Andropogon gerardii*

32 Blades basal, glossy green, usually convolute .. *Oryzopsis asperifolia*
   Blades erect or drooping, dull green, flat .. *Agropyron trachycaulum*
33 Emerging leaves folded 34
   Emerging leaves rolled 37
34 Plants aquatic; blades soft and flat .... *Catabrosa aquatica*
   Plants not aquatic; blades not soft 35
35 Ligule a fringe of hairs; sheath with
      scarious margins; plants sod-forming .... *Distichlis stricta*
   Ligule membranous; sheath with hyaline
      margins; plants tufted 36
36 Blades to 6 mm wide, rather lax, to 15 cm
      long; plants loosely tufted .... *Muhlenbergia racemosa*
   Blades to 2 mm wide, rather stiff, rarely
      more than 5 cm long; plants loosely
      tufted .... *Muhlenbergia asperifolia*
   Blades to 2 mm wide; rather stiff, to
      10 cm long; plants densely tufted ... *Muhlenbergia richardsonis*
37 Ligule a fringe of hairs .... *Spartina gracilis*
   Ligule membranous 38
38 Sheath closed in early stages, splitting in
      middle at maturity, purplish at base .. *Schizachne purpurascens*
   Sheath split 39
39 Sheath with scarious margins 40
   Sheath with hyaline margins 42
40 Plants with distinctive odor when crushed .... *Hierochloe odorata*
   Plants without odor when crushed 41
41 Blades rather lax, to 10 mm wide;
      collar glabrous .... *Calamagrostis canadensis*
   Blades lax, to 4 mm wide;
      collar pubescent .... *Calamagrostis rubescens*
   Blades stiff, to 4 mm wide;
      collar glabrous .... *Calamagrostis inexpansa*
42 Blades narrow, usually less than 5 mm wide 43
   Blades usually more than 5 mm wide 44
43 Plants of dry prairie; ligule acute, to 7 mm
      long; blades bluish green .... *Calamagrostis montanensis*
   Plants of marshland; ligule truncate,
      to 4 mm long; blades green .... *Calamagrostis neglecta*
44 Plants tufted; blades short, usually less than
      15 cm long; woodlands and moist prairie ..... *Phleum alpinum*
   Plants not tufted; blades to 50 cm long;
      moist prairie .... *Sorghastrum nutans*
   Plants not tufted; blades to 35 cm long;
      wetland and slough margins .... *Scolochloa festucacea*
45 Ligule a fringe of hairs or absent 46
   Ligule membranous 54
46 Blades 10 mm or more wide; annuals 47
   Blades less than 10 mm wide 49
47 Ligule absent; sheath compressed, keeled;
      shoots prostrate or ascending .... *Echinochloa crusgalli*
   Ligule present; sheath compressed or
      round; shoots erect 48

48 Sheath compressed, keeled, glabrous;
   blades pubescent at base .... *Setaria glauca*
   Sheath compressed, not keeled, pubescent;
   blades not pubescent at base .... *Setaria viridis*
   Sheath round, conspicuously pubescent;
   blades pubescent on both surfaces .... *Panicum capillare*
49 Plants annual, prostrate, mat-forming;
   blade to 3 cm long, stiff .... *Munroa squarrosa*
   Plants perennial, not prostrate;
   blade longer than 3 cm 50
50 Emerging leaves folded 51
   Emerging leaves rolled 53
51 Sheath margins hyaline; sheath long-pubescent;
   blades long-pubescent on lower surface,
   sparsely pubescent above .... *Danthonia intermedia*
   Sheath margins scarious; sheath and blades not as above 52
52 Plants pilose-pubescent; collar distinct, broad;
   blade narrow, to 15 cm long .... *Danthonia unispicata*
   Plants sparsely pubescent; collar indistinct,
   narrow; blade narrow, to 15 cm long, curled .. *Danthonia spicata*
   Plants almost glabrous; collar narrow;
   blades to 25 cm long .... *Danthonia parryi*
53 Plants usually decumbent, spreading; blades
   distinctly veined, tapering to a point ... *Sporobolus cryptandrus*
   Plants erect; blades not distinctly veined,
   bristle-like and often curled .... *Aristida longiseta*
54 Tips of blades boat-shaped 55
   Tips of blades not boat-shaped 60
55 Plants annual, low; shoots usually decumbent;
   blades short, often cross-wrinkled .... *Poa annua*
   Plants perennial, mostly erect 56
56 Plants short-stoloniferous; blades glossy light green .... *Poa trivialis*
   Plants not stoloniferous 57
57 Plants densely tufted 58
   Plants loosely tufted 59
58 Shoots very flat, broad; blades flat to
   folded, erect, to 5 mm wide, light green;
   ligule to 5 mm long .... *Helicotrichon hookeri*
   Shoots not very flat, small; blades folded,
   often bristle-like, to 3 mm wide, dark bluish-
   green; ligule to 1 mm long .... *Poa cusickii*
   Shoots not very flat, small; blades flat to
   folded, to 2 mm wide, green; ligule to 3 mm long .. *Poa secunda*
59 Plants tall, decumbent at base; blades lax, broad
   at base .... *Poa palustris*
   Plants not tall, not decumbent at base; blades
   stiff, linear .... *Poa canbyi*
60 Emerging leaves folded 61
   Emerging leaves rolled 67
61 Ligule conspicuous, to 10 mm long 62
   Ligule inconspicuous, to 1 mm long 63

23

62 Blades to 10 mm wide, flat, long,
    indistinctly veined .... *Dactylis glomerata*
   Blades to 5 mm wide, flat, long, prominently
    veined, translucent between veins ..... *Deschampsia caespitosa*
   Blades to 2 mm wide, short, flexuous,
    indistinctly veined .... *Schedonnardus paniculatus*
63 Blades flat to folded or involute 64
   Blades filiform 65
64 Plants with hard, bulb-like bases; blades tapering to a
    fine point, dull green; collar glabrous .. *Muhlenbergia cuspidata*
   Plants without bulb-like bases; blades mostly linear,
    acuminate, bluish-green; collar pubescent .... *Koeleria cristata*
   Plants without bulb-like bases; blades mostly linear,
    acute, dark green; collar glabrous .... *Festuca scabrella*
65 Plants annual, not densely tufted .... *Festuca octoflora*
   Plants perennial, densely tufted 66
66 Plants bluish or gray green; veins indistinct;
    blades to 25 cm long .... *Festuca idahoensis*
   Plants bluish or gray green; veins distinct;
    blades to 15 cm long .... *Festuca ovina*
   Plants dark green; veins distinct;
    blades to 50 cm long .... *Festuca scabrella*
67 Ligule conspicuous, usually more than 3 mm long 68
   Ligule inconspicuous, less than 3 mm long 75
68 Plants ascending from spreading base;
    stoloniferous .... *Agrostis stolonifera*
   Plants not stoloniferous 69
69 Sheath margins scarious 70
   Sheath margins hyaline 71
70 Plants often densely tufted, erect, bluish
    green; blades indistinctly veined;
    saline and alkaline habitats .... *Puccinellia nuttalliana*
   Plants not densely tufted, often decumbent, dull green;
    blades distinctly veined; wet habitats ..... *Alopecurus aequalis*
71 Plants annual; blades to 12 mm wide, twisted
    near tip; dry habitats .... *Phalaris canariensis*
   Plants annual; blades to 12 mm wide, not
    twisted near tip; wet habitats .... *Beckmannia syzigachne*
   Plants perennial 72
72 Blades to 12 mm wide, lax; sheath prominently
    veined, purplish at base .... *Cinna latifolia*
   Blades to 5 mm wide 73
73 Plants of moist habitats; blades indistinctly
    veined, flat, thin .... *Sphenopholis obtusata*
   Plants of dry habitats; blades distinctly
    veined, flat or involute, firm 74
74 Blades usually strongly involute, very long;
    ligule very conspicuous, to 8 mm long ... *Oryzopsis hymenoides*
   Blades flat to involute or convolute; ligule
    conspicuous, obtuse or truncate, to 4 mm long .... *Stipa comata*
   Blades flat to involute or convolute; ligule

DESCRIPTIONS OF SPECIES

The order of entry is alphabetical by botanical name. An index to common names begins on page 236.

AGROHORDEUM MACOUNII (Vasey) Lepage

Macoun's wild rye, tufted wild rye

Growth habit	erect, densely tufted, perennial, with fibrous roots
Blade	to 5 mm wide, 5 to 20 cm long, erect, rather firm, flat to involute, acuminate, usually scabrous on both sides; midvein extending partway down sheath; rolled at emergence
Sheath	round, split, retrorsely pubescent to glabrate, often purplish at base; veins prominent; margins hyaline
Ligule	to 1 mm long, membranous, truncate, ciliate
Collar	very often indistinct, divided, light or brownish green, glabrous
Auricles	absent or rudimentary
Where found	throughout area, in moist meadows and borders of woods
Remarks	a natural sterile hybrid of *Agropyron trachycaulum* and *Hordeum jubatum*

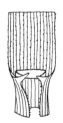 

AGROPYRON CRISTATUM (L.) Gaertn.

crested wheat grass

Growth habit	perennial, tufted, with a dense mass of fibrous roots
Blade	to 8 mm wide, 5 to 20 cm long, flat or slightly involute, acuminate, scabrous and often soft-pubescent on upper surface, smooth or slightly scabrous on lower surface; veins prominent; midvein light-colored; margins scabrous; rolled at emergence
Sheath	round, split, smooth, slightly scabrous or lowest sheaths often soft-pubescent; margins overlapping, hyaline
Ligule	to 1.5 mm long, membranous, truncate, lacerate
Collar	divided, distinct, light or yellowish green, smooth to ciliate
Auricles	to 1.5 mm long, clawlike
Where found	seeded in various soil types because of its drought tolerance
Remarks	introduced; the closely related desert wheat grass, *Agropyron desertorum* (Fisch.) Schutt., has no pubescence on the upper surface of the leaves

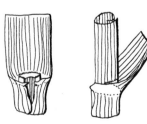

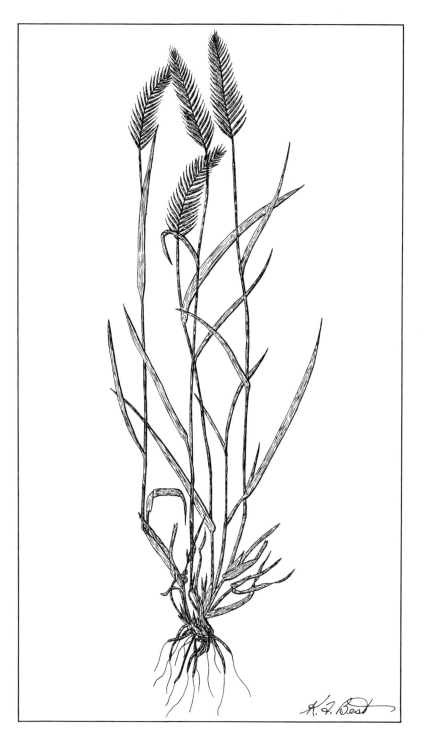

AGROPYRON DASYSTACHYUM (Hook.) Scribn.

northern wheat grass

Growth habit	perennial, with rhizomes
Blade	to 6 mm wide, 5 to 20 cm long, flat to involute; ridged and very scabrous on upper surface, smooth or sometimes scabrous near base on lower surface; margins scabrous; rolled at emergence
Sheath	round, split, smooth or slightly scabrous; midrib often continuing partway down; margins overlapping, scarious
Ligule	to 1 mm long, membranous, obtuse, lacerate
Collar	divided, smooth, light green
Auricles	to 2 mm long, clawlike, clasping, slender
Where found	throughout entire area; the most common wheat grass on the Prairies
Remarks	awned northern wheat grass, *Agropyron albicans* Scribn. & Smith, a close relative, has narrower leaves

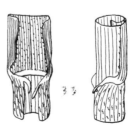

AGROPYRON ELONGATUM (Host) Beauv.

tall wheat grass

Growth habit	tall, erect, loosely tufted, perennial, with fibrous roots
Blade	to 10 mm wide and 20 cm long, appearing glabrous but actually minutely puberulent, acuminate; midrib prominent near collar; rolled at emergence
Sheath	round, split; margins overlapping, hyaline
Ligule	less than 1 mm long, membranous, serrate, often turned downward
Collar	to 2 mm wide, yellow
Auricles	small, clasping, often not seen on older leaves
Where found	hayfields and pastures throughout the area on saline soil
Remarks	introduced by the University of Saskatchewan in 1929 from Siberia; the most salt-tolerant of all cultivated grasses

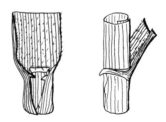

AGROPYRON INTERMEDIUM (Host) Beauv.

intermediate wheat grass

Growth habit	erect, perennial, with short rhizomes
Blade	to 10 mm wide, 5 to 15 cm long, flat, light green, usually glabrous but pubescent in some strains; midvein prominent on back; margins ciliate; rolled at emergence
Sheath	outer margin usually ciliate, inner margin hyaline
Ligule	less than 1 mm long, serrate
Collar	to 2 mm wide, yellow, continuous
Auricles	variable, slender, clasping, often rudimentary
Where found	fairly common in hayfields and pastures in the Parkland
Remarks	introduced; often short-lived when grazed; palatable to all classes of livestock; pubescence on blade varies considerably; the introduced pubescent wheat grass, *Agropyron trichophorum* (Link) Richt., has similar vegetative characters

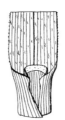

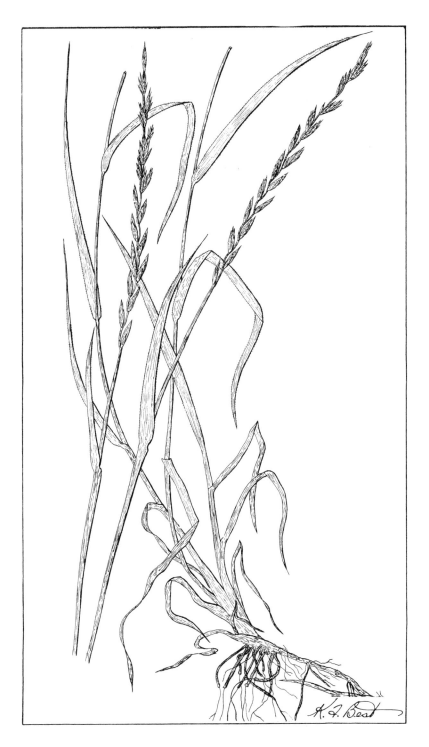

AGROPYRON REPENS (L.) Beauv.

quack grass, couch grass

Growth habit	erect, sod-forming, perennial, with long yellowish white rhizomes
Blade	to 10 mm wide, 6 to 20 cm long, flat or U-shaped, acuminate, slightly keeled at base, green, sometimes glaucous; harsh-scabrous on margins and upper surface, usually sparsely pilose; smooth on lower surface; twisted near tip; rolled at emergence
Sheath	round, split, short, lower sheaths usually pubescent; margins overlapping, hyaline
Ligule	to 1 mm long, membranous, obtuse, entire, lacerate or sometimes ciliate
Collar	divided, distinct, broad, puberulent, yellowish or sometimes tinged with purple
Auricles	to 3 mm long, clawlike, slender
Where found	a weed of waste places and gardens; occasionally in cultivated fields
Remarks	introduced; considerable variation occurs in pubescence of this species; young plants and spring growth are usually more pubescent than older plants or growth produced later in the season. *Agropyron repens* may be distinguished from *Agropyron cristatum* by the puberulent collar and lesser degree of ridging on the leaves. *A. repens* is not tufted, *A. cristatum* is strongly tufted

AGROPYRON SMITHII Rydb.

western wheat grass, bluejoint

Growth habit	erect, sod-forming, perennial, with long slender rhizomes
Blade	to 6 mm wide, 5 to 25 cm long, flat or involute, stiff, acuminate; prominently ridged and scabrous (rarely pubescent) on upper surface, smooth on lower surface; glaucous, bluish green; margins scabrous; blade attached at 45-degree angle to stem; rolled at emergence
Sheath	round, split, prominently veined, glabrous, sometimes brown or purplish at base; margins scarious
Ligule	to 0.5 mm long, membranous, truncate, lacerate, or ciliate
Collar	continuous, medium-broad, not well defined, glabrous, light green, sometimes oblique
Auricles	claw-shaped, clasping, sometimes purplish at base
Where found	throughout area on heavy soils; tolerates drought as well as adequate moisture; alkali-tolerant

AGROPYRON SPICATUM (Pursh) Scribn. & Smith

bluebunch wheat grass

Growth habit	erect, bunch-forming, densely tufted, perennial, with fibrous roots
Blade	to 5 mm wide, 5 to 20 cm long, flat to convolute, ridged; scabrous and hirsute on upper surface, with prominent midrib and veins on lower surface, often minutely pubescent between veins; rolled at emergence
Sheath	round, split, strongly veined, glabrous; margins overlapping, scarious
Ligule	to 0.5 mm long, membranous, truncate, lacerate
Collar	continuous or sometimes divided, glabrous, yellowish
Auricles	to 1.5 mm long; rudimentary to clawlike and fragile if present
Where found	dry prairie in western part of area; common in south central British Columbia

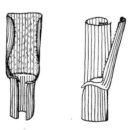

K. d. Best.

AGROPYRON SUBSECUNDUM (Link) Hitchc.

awned wheat grass

Growth habit	erect, tufted, perennial, with fibrous roots
Blade	to 10 mm wide, 4 to 20 cm long, flat or involute, acuminate; ridged and scabrous on upper surface, slightly scabrous on lower surface; pubescent when young; margins white and very scabrous; rolled at emergence
Sheath	round, split, glabrous in old plants, densely pubescent when young, prominently veined, light green; margins scarious
Ligule	to 1 mm long, membranous, obtuse to truncate, lacerate, brownish
Collar	divided, well defined, light brown
Auricles	absent, or if present, clawlike and often only one
Where found	throughout area, but more common on moist prairie and at forest margins

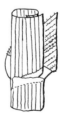

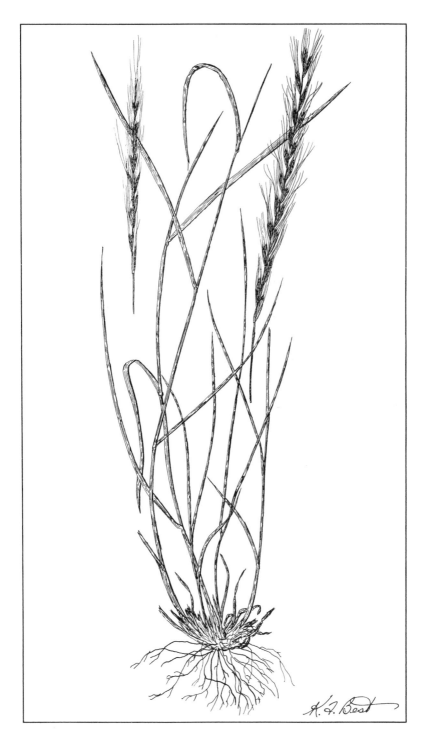

AGROPYRON TRACHYCAULUM (Link) Malte

slender wheat grass, western rye grass

Growth habit	erect, tufted, perennial, with very short rhizomes
Blade	to 6 mm wide, 5 to 25 cm long, flat, narrowed at base, acuminate, medium green, glaucous; ridged and scabrous on upper surface, keeled and slightly scabrous on lower surface; margins strongly scabrous; rolled at emergence
Sheath	round, split, glabrous, light green, white or purplish at base; margins hyaline
Ligule	to 1 mm long, membranous, truncate, finely ciliate
Collar	continuous, distinct, glabrous, yellowish green, often oblique
Auricles	rudimentary or absent; often only one
Where found	throughout area; the most common wheat grass in situations with good moisture
Remarks	grown for hay for many years before 1940; presently being improved in a plant breeding program; tolerates saline soil

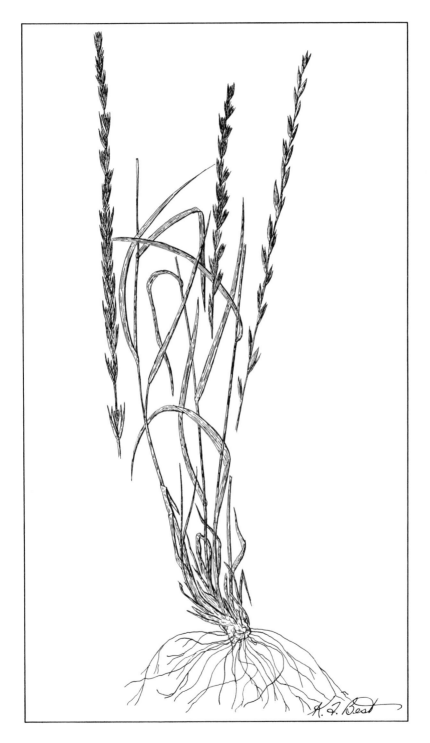

AGROSTIS PALUSTRIS Huds.

creeping bent

Growth habit	stoloniferous, prostrate, perennial, branching and rooting at the nodes, mat-forming
Blade	to 4 mm wide, 3 to 10 cm long, flat, tapering, erect; distinctly ridged on upper surface, slightly keeled on lower surface, scabrous on both surfaces and on margins; rolled at emergence
Sheath	round, split, glabrous, pale green or purplish; margins hyaline
Ligule	to 3 mm long, membranous, thin, entire or finely lacerate, minutely hairy on back
Collar	distinct, smooth, pale green, usually oblique
Auricles	absent
Where found	throughout area in moist places; not common

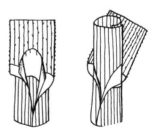

K.A. Best.

AGROSTIS SCABRA Willd.

hair grass, tickle grass, flyaway grass, rough hair grass

Growth habit	tufted, perennial, with fibrous roots
Blade	to 2 mm wide, 2 to 8 cm long, soft, acuminate, often inrolled or involute and hairlike when dry, glabrous; distinctly ridged and scabrous on upper surface, smooth and distinctly keeled on under surface; margins scabrous; rolled at emergence
Sheath	round, slightly keeled, glabrous, smooth, pale green to white or purplish, split; margins overlapping
Ligule	to 3 mm long, membranous, truncate or three-pointed, entire or finely lacerate, hairy on outer surface
Collar	narrow, inconspicuous, pale green
Auricles	absent
Where found	throughout area, but common only on moist prairie; one of the first invaders on abandoned farmland

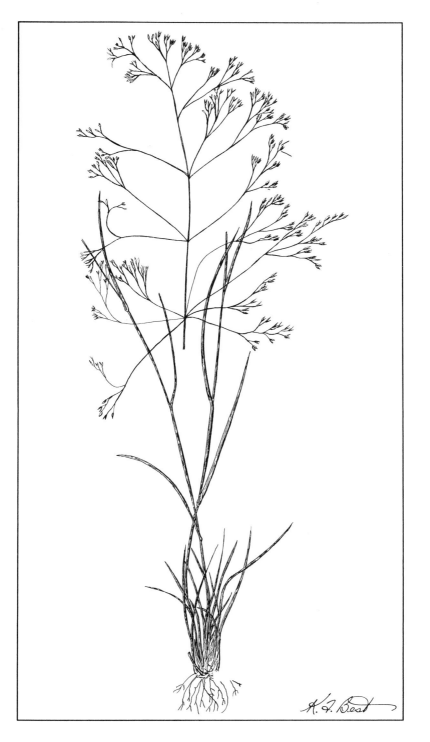

AGROSTIS STOLONIFERA L.

redtop

Growth habit	perennial, with fibrous roots; ascending from a spreading base, the decumbent portion rooting at nodes in wet soil
Blade	to 3 mm wide, flat, deep green; rolled at emergence
Sheath	round, split
Ligule	to 5 mm long, hairy on back, membranous
Collar	continuous, pale green
Auricles	absent or rudimentary
Where found	seeded in lawns, on golf courses, and on landing strips
Remarks	introduced

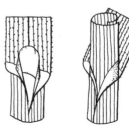

ALOPECURUS AEQUALIS Sobol.

short-awned foxtail

Growth habit	low, erect, tufted, glabrous, perennial, with fibrous roots
Blade	to 5 mm wide, 4 to 15 cm long, flat, acuminate, dull green, both surfaces and margins scabrous; rolled at emergence
Sheath	round, split, glabrous, green, often purplish at base, with light veins; margins scarious
Ligule	to 5 mm long, membranous, obtuse, minutely pubescent on back, particularly at base
Collar	medium broad, divided, oblique, glabrous, light brown
Auricles	absent
Where found	throughout area around sloughs, springs, and streams; also along roadsides and in shady places in north

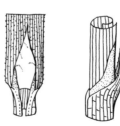

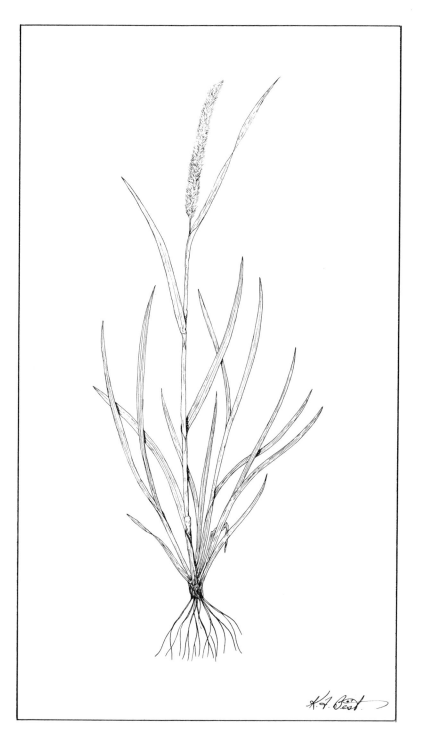

ALOPECURUS PRATENSIS L.

meadow foxtail

Growth habit	erect, perennial, forming loose tufts, with very short stolons
Blade	to 6 mm wide, 5 to 15 cm long, flat, acuminate; ridged and scabrous on upper surface, slightly keeled and scaberulous or smooth below; margins very scabrous; rolled at emergence
Sheath	round, split, glabrous, green, often purplish at base, lower sheaths loose, upper ones often inflated; margins overlapping, broad, hyaline
Ligule	to 3 mm long, coarse-membranous, obtuse or truncate, entire, undulate, oblique, faintly striate, ciliate, puberulent on back, variable in shape and margin
Collar	divided, often oblique, glabrous, yellowish
Auricles	absent
Where found	low moist areas and waste places
Remarks	introduced; not common

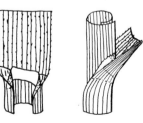

ANDROPOGON GERARDII Vitman

big bluestem

Growth habit	tall, erect, perennial, with short, thick, scaly rhizomes
Blade	to 10 mm wide, 8 to 50 cm long, flat or V-shaped, constricted at base, acuminate, extending partway down the sheath, slightly scabrous or smooth above, smooth below, with silky hairs at base, light green and often red-tinged, especially near the tip; veins distinct, midvein prominent; margins scabrous; rolled at emergence
Sheath	compressed, split, usually purplish at base and below ground, soft-pubescent or sometimes glabrous; veins distinct; margins hyaline
Ligule	to 3 mm long, membranous, obtuse, ciliate and often lacerate
Collar	medium broad, often indistinct, light or yellowish green, sometimes divided by midvein, pubescent at least on margins
Auricles	absent
Where found	eastern part of area and as far west as the Qu'Appelle Valley; one of the most important species of the true prairie; to 4 feet tall

ANDROPOGON SCOPARIUS Michx.

little bluestem

Growth habit	erect, tufted, perennial, with short scaly rhizomes
Blade	to 8 mm wide, 5 to 15 cm long, flat to folded, constricted at base; scabrous on upper surface and margins, smooth below; light green, often red-tinged, sometimes glistening, often glaucous; little twisted, tip blunt; folded at emergence
Sheath	compressed, keeled, split, quite open in older leaves, smooth or scabrous, often purplish at base
Ligule	to 2 mm long, membranous, obtuse to truncate, ciliate
Collar	continuous, broad, glabrous, light green or pinkish
Auricles	absent
Where found	throughout area; in Manitoba an important grass of true prairie, westward becoming restricted to areas of adequate moisture or high water table

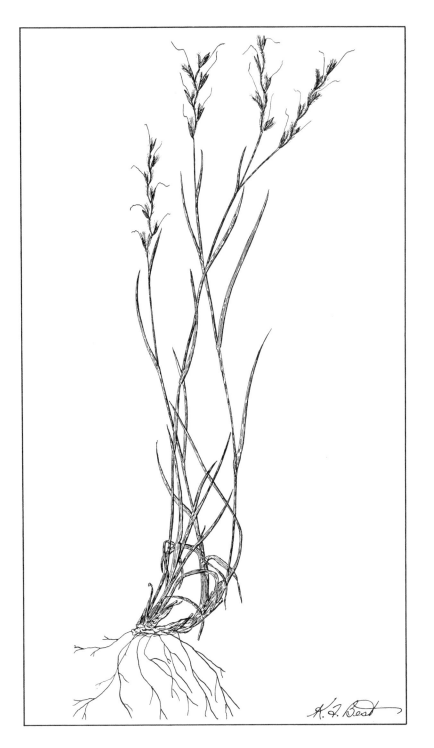

ARISTIDA LONGISETA Steud.

red three-awn

Growth habit	densely tufted, perennial, with fibrous roots
Blade	to 2 mm wide, 3 to 15 cm long, bristle-like or involute, often curved or flexuous, both surfaces and margins very scabrous upwardly; veins not very distinct; rolled at emergence
Sheath	round, split, prominently veined, having upward-pointing minute prickles, sometimes smooth; margins overlapping, hyaline
Ligule	to 0.5 mm long, a fringe of fine hairs
Collar	indistinct, continuous, retrorsely scabrous, whitish green when evident, with tufts of long hairs at margins
Auricles	absent
Where found	western part of area only; gravelly slopes and dry prairie
Remarks	rare

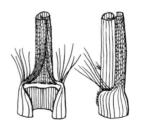

BECKMANNIA SYZIGACHNE (Steud.) Fern.

slough grass

Growth habit	erect, tufted, annual or biennial, forming large bunches, with fibrous roots
Blade	to 12 mm wide, 8 to 20 cm long, flat, more or less stiff, scabrous above, smooth below; midvein present but not prominent; rolled at emergence
Sheath	round, split, glabrous, smooth; venation muriform; margins overlapping, hyaline
Ligule	to 10 mm long, membranous, obtuse, often lacerate at tip when old
Collar	inconspicuous, divided, smooth, brown or yellowish
Auricles	absent
Where found	in and around shallow sloughs and wet meadows throughout area

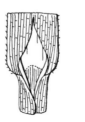

BOUTELOUA CURTIPENDULA (Michx.) Torr.

side-oat grama

Growth habit	erect, sod-forming, perennial, with short scaly rhizomes
Blade	to 7 mm wide, 5 to 30 cm long, flat to convolute, acuminate, little twisted, scabrous above, smooth below, with few long hairs scattered on both surfaces; veins distinct; margins scabrous to ciliate; rolled at emergence
Sheath	round, split, usually pubescent, often purplish at the base; veins prominent; margins hyaline
Ligule	to 1 mm long, membranous, truncate, lacerate, ciliate
Collar	medium broad, yellowish green or brown, continuous, with few hairs at the throat
Auricles	absent
Where found	southeastern Saskatchewan along the Souris River and in southwestern Manitoba; rare in Canada

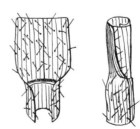

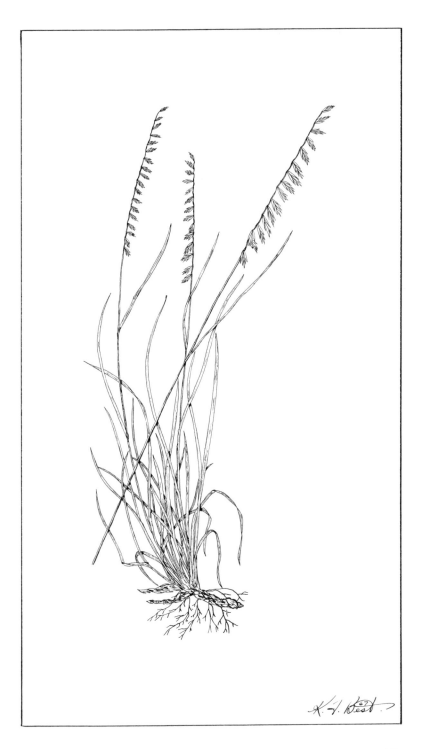

BOUTELOUA GRACILIS (H.B.K.) Lag. ex Steud.

blue grama

Growth habit	densely tufted, perennial, with fibrous roots; occasionally with very short scaly rhizomes
Blade	to 3 mm wide, 2 to 15 cm long, flat to convolute, acuminate, light to medium green, curled; scabrous or pubescent on upper surface especially near base, glabrous on lower surface; veins prominent above and below; rolled at emergence
Sheath	round, split, veins distinct; glabrous or sparsely pilose; margins hyaline
Ligule	to 0.5 mm long; a dense fringe of hairs
Collar	continuous, medium-broad, distinctly yellowish green, with long hairs on inside of margins
Auricles	absent
Where found	throughout area on dry prairie
Remarks	commonly associated with *Stipa comata;* less common northward

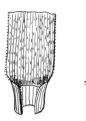

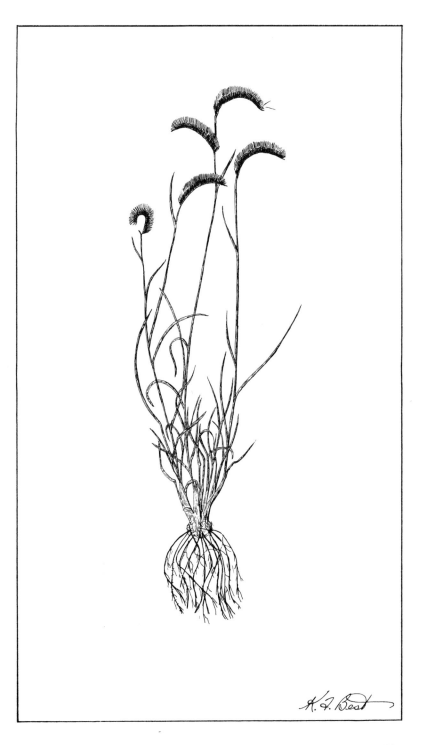

BROMUS CARINATUS Hook. & Arn.

California brome

Growth habit	erect, annual or biennial, with fibrous roots
Blade	to 8 mm wide, to 30 cm long, flat, tapering, prominently veined and pilose on both surfaces; margins scabrous; rolled at emergence
Sheath	slightly compressed to round, split partway, retrorsely pilose, rarely glabrous; veins prominent, midvein continuing down the sheath
Ligule	to 2 mm long, membranous, longitudinally corrugated, obtuse, lacerate
Collar	indistinct, very narrow, divided, brownish green
Auricles	absent
Where found	throughout area in open woods and disturbed places; rare

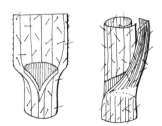

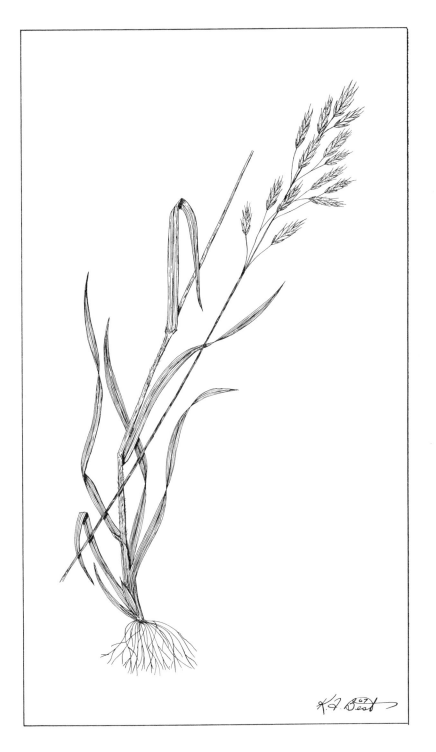

71

BROMUS CILIATUS L.

fringed brome

Growth habit	tall, perennial, with fibrous roots
Blade	to 10 mm wide, 8 to 20 cm long, flat, acuminate, dark green, glabrous or soft-pubescent; veins prominent on both surfaces, whitish midvein on lower side extending partway down the sheath; margins scabrous; rolled at emergence
Sheath	round, closed to near top, prominently veined, retrorsely pilose or glabrous in older leaves
Ligule	to about 1 mm long, coarse-membranous, truncate, entire or lacerate
Collar	divided, narrow, glabrous, pale green or brownish; margins sometimes constricted
Auricles	absent
Where found	throughout the Parkland and the Cypress Hills in fescue prairie and forest margins

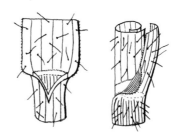

BROMUS INERMIS Leyss.

smooth brome

Growth habit	tall, perennial, with rhizomes
Blade	to 12 mm wide, 15 to 40 cm long, flat, acuminate, dark green, usually glabrous on both surfaces but sometimes minutely pubescent; veins and midrib distinct below; margins scabrous; rolled at emergence
Sheath	round, closed to near the top, prominently veined, usually glabrous, sometimes scabrous
Ligule	to 1 mm long, membranous, obtuse, entire or lacerate, often brownish at base
Collar	narrow, continuous or divided by midvein, glabrous, light or yellowish green
Auricles	absent or rarely rudimentary
Where found	throughout the entire area, but more commonly in the Parkland
Remarks	introduced; the common cultivated brome; known as Austrian brome when introduced into Canada about 1875

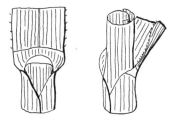

BROMUS PUMPELLIANUS Scribn.

northern awnless brome

Growth habit	erect, sod-forming, perennial; with strong, creeping, scaly rhizomes
Blade	to 12 mm wide, 10 to 25 cm long, flat, acuminate; veins distinct and very scabrous below, midrib extending partway down sheath; margins scarious and very scabrous; rolled at emergence
Sheath	round, closed to near the top, prominently veined, smooth or scabrous, often purplish at base
Ligule	to 3 mm long, membranous, brown, truncate, lacerate
Collar	continuous, narrow, glabrous, yellowish or light green
Auricles	absent or occasionally rudimentary
Where found	throughout Parkland and Cypress Hills at forest margins and on moist prairie

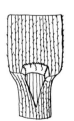

BROMUS TECTORUM L.

downy brome, downy chess

Growth habit	tufted, annual, with fibrous roots
Blade	to 8 mm wide, 5 to 12 cm long, flat, softly pubescent, sharp-pointed, pale green; margins pilose; rolled at emergence
Sheath	not compressed, keeled, softly pubescent, pale green, often pink- or purple-tinged, split only partway
Ligule	to 3 mm long, membranous, truncate, lacerate
Collar	pubescent, pale, narrow, distinct, usually divided
Auricles	absent
Where found	western part of area; common in British Columbia
Remarks	a troublesome weed in overgrazed pastures and waste places

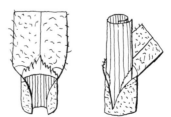

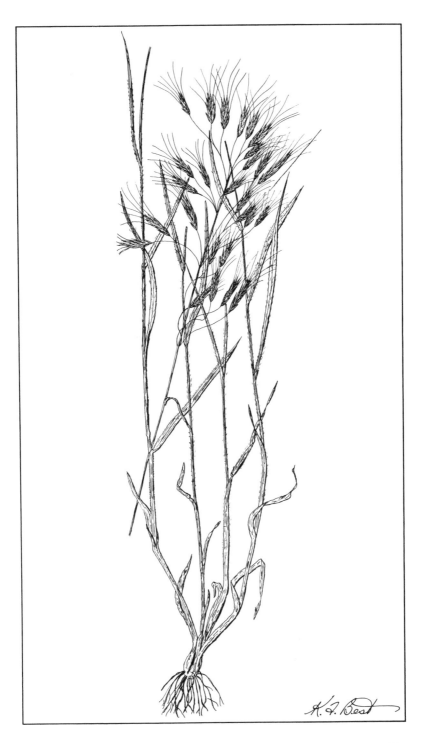

CALAMAGROSTIS CANADENSIS (Michx.) Beauv.

marsh reed grass

Growth habit	tall, erect, tufted, perennial, with rhizomes
Blade	to 10 mm wide, 7 to 40 cm long, flat, lax, medium green, acuminate; ridged and scabrous above, midrib prominent, smooth or slightly scabrous below; margins scabrous; rolled at emergence
Sheath	round, split, with scarious margins, distinctly veined, glabrous, yellowish at the base
Ligule	to 5 mm long, membranous, truncate, lacerate, often irregular or split
Collar	indistinct, continuous or divided, glabrous, yellowish green, often oblique
Auricles	absent
Where found	throughout entire area in swamps and sloughs

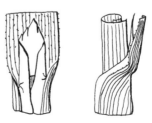

CALAMAGROSTIS INEXPANSA A. Gray

northern reed grass

Growth habit	tall, erect, tufted, perennial, with slender rhizomes
Blade	to 4 mm wide, 10 to 30 cm long, flat or involute, convolute in young shoots, firm; ridged and very scabrous above, smooth or slightly scabrous below; medium to light green; margins scabrous; rolled at emergence
Sheath	round or slightly compressed, split, with scarious overlapping margins, prominently veined, sometimes purplish at base
Ligule	to 6 mm long, membranous, obtuse or truncate, lacerate or slightly ciliate
Collar	indistinct, continuous or divided, glabrous, yellowish green, often oblique
Auricles	absent
Where found	throughout area in wet places and meadows

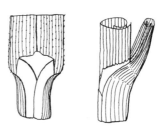

83

CALAMAGROSTIS MONTANENSIS Scribn.

plains reed grass

Growth habit	erect, sod-forming, perennial, with slender rhizomes
Blade	to 3 mm wide, 5 to 20 cm long, bluish green, stiff, flat to involute, acuminate, veins prominent; ridged and scabrous on the upper surface, faintly midribbed and scabrous below; margins scabrous; rolled at emergence
Sheath	round, split, with hyaline margins, prominently veined with midrib extending down the sheath, light green, slightly scabrous
Ligule	to 7 mm long, membranous, acute, entire or lacerate in older leaves
Collar	indistinct, glabrous, light or brownish green
Auricles	absent
Where found	throughout northern part of area on dry to moderately moist prairie; occasionally throughout southern Saskatchewan and Alberta

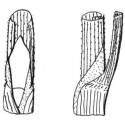

CALAMAGROSTIS NEGLECTA (Ehrh.) Gaertn. Mey. & Schreb.

narrow reed grass

Growth habit	erect, perennial, with long slender rhizomes
Blade	to 5 mm wide, 8 to 30 cm long, flat to convolute, acuminate, ridged and scabrous above, smooth or scabrous below, glaucous, green, usually erect; mid-vein indistinct; margins scabrous; rolled at emergence
Sheath	round, split, with hyaline margins, distinctly veined, glabrous, white or purplish below
Ligule	to 4 mm long, membranous, truncate, lacerate and ciliate
Collar	indistinct, narrow, continuous, glabrous, light or yellowish green
Auricles	absent
Where found	throughout area in wet places
Remarks	usually associated with *C. canadensis* and *C. inexpansa,* but much less common

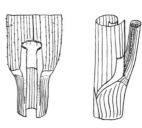

CALAMAGROSTIS RUBESCENS Buckl.

pine grass

Growth habit	erect, sod-forming, perennial, with extensive rhizomes
Blade	to 4 mm wide, 10 to 30 cm long, flat or involute, lax, upper and lower surfaces scaberulous; margins scabrous; rolled at emergence
Sheath	round, split, with scarious margins, distinctly veined, often purplish at base, scabrous
Ligule	to 4 mm long, membranous, obtuse or acute, lacerate when old
Collar	distinct, divided by midrib, pubescent with long soft hairs
Auricles	absent
Where found	western coniferous forests, Cypress Hills, and locally in boreal forests, very common in central British Columbia

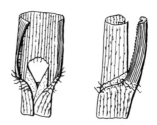

CALAMOVILFA LONGIFOLIA (Hook.) Scribn.

sand reed grass

Growth habit	tall, erect, perennial, with long scaly rhizomes
Blade	to 12 mm wide, 10 to 50 cm long, flat to involute, firm, coriaceous, acuminate, smooth on both surfaces, light green; veins not prominent; margins scarious and slightly scabrous; rolled at emergence
Sheath	round, split, distinctly veined, usually smooth but sometimes slightly scabrous or pubescent, light green, often pinkish at base; margins overlapping, hyaline
Ligule	to 3 mm long; a fringe of hairs
Collar	distinct, broad, continuous, yellowish, with tufts of fine hairs on inner margins
Auricles	absent
Where found	throughout entire area on sandy soils
Remarks	one of the most important grasses in sand hills; usually associated with *Sporobolus cryptandrus* and *Oryzopsis hymenoides*

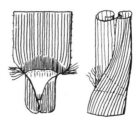

CATABROSA AQUATICA (L.) Beauv.

brook grass

Growth habit	perennial, with elongated rhizomes; rooting from prostrate stems
Blade	to 8 mm wide, usually less than 10 cm long, obtuse, flat and flaccid, smooth on both sides, with fine midvein; folded at emergence
Sheath	round or slightly compressed, split partway, smooth, and often purplish at base; margins hyaline
Ligule	to 8 mm long, membranous, obtuse
Collar	distinct, narrow, continuous, glabrous, lighter or darker green than leaf blade
Auricles	absent
Where found	throughout area in shallow streams and springs, but not common

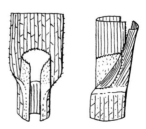

CINNA LATIFOLIA (Trev.) Griseb.

slender wood grass

Growth habit	tall, slightly tufted, perennial, with fibrous roots; sometimes bulbous at base
Blade	to 12 mm wide, 10 to 25 cm long, flat, acuminate, finely scabrous on both surfaces; midvein present, extending partway down sheath; rolled at emergence
Sheath	round, split, prominently veined, purplish at base, smooth; margins overlapping, hyaline
Ligule	to 10 mm long, membranous, obtuse, usually lacerate
Collar	divided, distinct, purplish or dark brown, glabrous
Auricles	absent
Where found	throughout area in moist forests

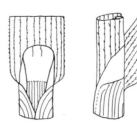

DACTYLIS GLOMERATA L.

orchard grass, cock's-foot

Growth habit	tall, smooth, tufted, perennial, with fibrous roots
Blade	to 10 mm wide, 5 to 25 cm long, flat to folded, tapering, pale green, often glaucous; veins indistinct above and below but with deep furrow over prominent and scabrous midrib; margins scarious, very scabrous; folded at emergence
Sheath	flattened, keeled, split partway, finely but distinctly veined, glabrous, pale green or purplish
Ligule	to 8 mm long, membranous, truncate, and bristle-tipped or obtuse, often split or lacerate, ciliolate
Collar	divided, broad, glabrous, yellowish
Auricles	absent
Where found	seeded in irrigated pastures and orchards; found growing wild in favorable locations
Remarks	introduced

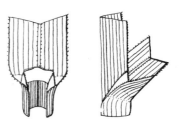

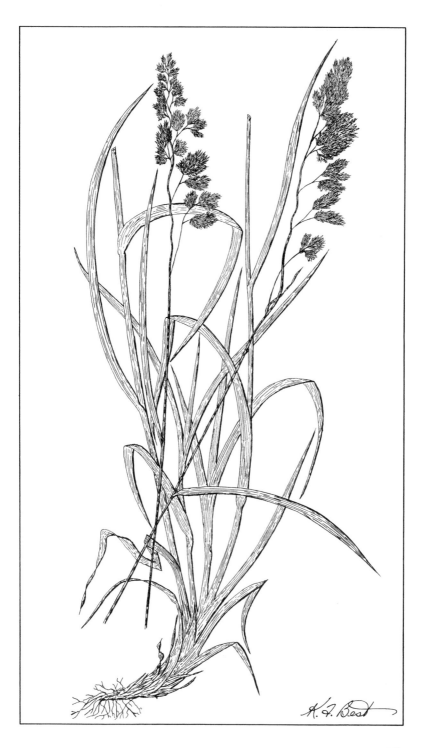

K. F. Best

DANTHONIA INTERMEDIA Vasey

wild oat grass, timber oat grass

Growth habit	short, tufted, perennial, with fibrous roots
Blade	to 3 mm wide, 5 to 15 cm long, flat to involute, acuminate; somewhat ridged and glabrous or sparsely hairy on upper surface, long-pubescent on lower surface; margins scarious and very slightly scabrous; folded at emergence
Sheath	round, split, with hyaline margins, pale green, prominently veined, very pilose-pubescent
Ligule	to 1 mm long; a fringe of hairs
Collar	distinct, narrow, yellowish green, continuous, with long hairs all around and on inner margins
Auricles	absent
Where found	Wood Mountain, Cypress Hills, Parkland, foothills of the Rocky Mountains; rare in western Manitoba

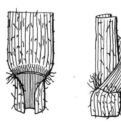

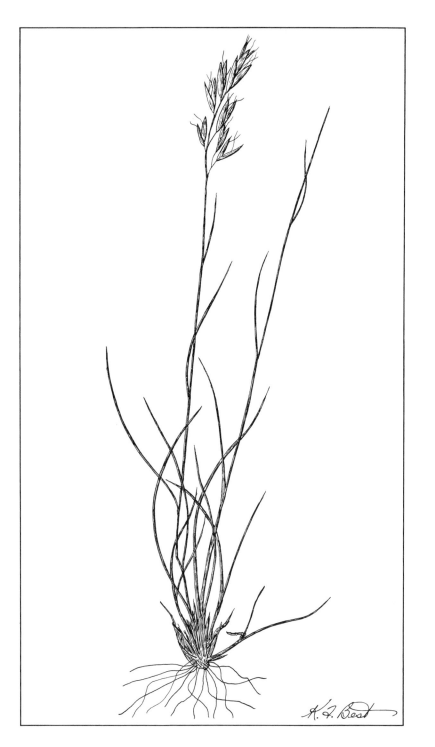

99

DANTHONIA PARRYI Scribn.

Parry oat grass

Growth habit	erect, densely tufted, perennial, with fibrous roots
Blade	to 3 mm wide, 10 to 25 cm long, flat to involute, mostly erect-flexuous and narrow or filiform, scaberulous on upper surface and on the scarious margins, glabrous below, yellowish green; veins distinct above but no midrib evident; folded at emergence
Sheath	round, split, distinctly ridged at the upper end, yellowish and glabrous; margins overlapping, scarious
Ligule	to 0.5 mm long; a fringe of hairs
Collar	a narrow dark continuous ridge, with tufts of long stiff hairs at margins
Auricles	absent
Where found	foothills of the Rocky Mountains as far north as Rocky Mountain House, rarer north of the Bow River
Remarks	blades break off at the collar during the winter

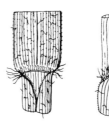

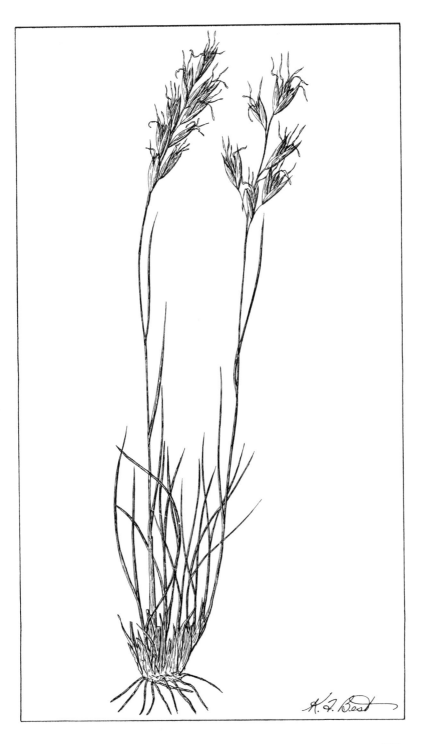

DANTHONIA SPICATA (L.) Beauv. ex Roem. & Schult.

poverty oat grass

Growth habit	tufted, perennial, with fibrous roots
Blade	to 3 mm wide, basal leaves 5 to 15 cm long, flat to convolute, acuminate, flexuous, usually sparsely pilose but often glabrous; prominently veined on both surfaces, under surface bright green and sometimes glossy, upper surface dull green or glaucous; margins scabrous; folded and involute at emergence
Sheath	round, split, with scarious margins, pale green to white, usually pilose-pubescent
Ligule	to 1.2 mm long; a fringe of hairs
Collar	narrow, continuous, often indistinct, light or yellowish green with long hairs at margins
Auricles	absent
Where found	throughout area, in moderately dry prairie but not common; occasionally abundant

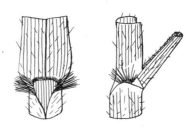

DANTHONIA UNISPICATA (Thurb.) Munro ex Macoun

one-spike oat grass, dwarf oat grass

Growth habit	short, erect, tufted, perennial, with fibrous roots
Blade	to 3 mm wide, 5 to 15 cm long, flat to involute, light green, pilose above, glabrous or slightly pilose below, light green, acuminate; margins scarious and scabrous; veins not very prominent; folded at emergence
Sheath	round, split, prominently veined; glabrous or upper sheaths pilose; margins overlapping, scarious
Ligule	a fringe of fine hairs
Collar	distinct, broad, flared up the blade, continuous, yellowish, with tufts of long hairs at margins
Auricles	absent
Where found	western part of area, in moderately dry prairie; not common

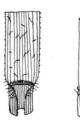

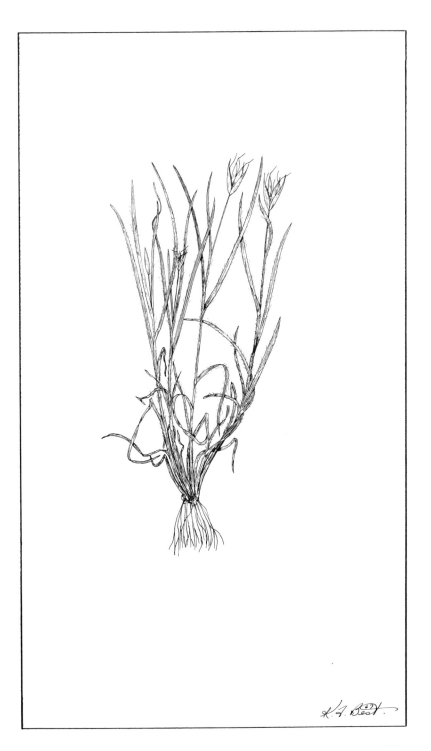

K. A. Best.

DESCHAMPSIA CAESPITOSA (L.) Beauv.

tufted hair grass

Growth habit	erect, densely tufted, perennial, with fibrous roots
Blade	to 5 mm wide, 5 to 30 cm long, flat to folded, rather firm and bristle-like, contracted at collar, often flexuous, prominently ridged and scabrous above, smooth or slightly scabrous below; translucent between veins, light green; margins scabrous; folded at emergence
Sheath	compressed, keeled, prominently veined, split, light green or straw-colored; margins overlapping, hyaline
Ligule	to 10 mm long, membranous, acuminate, entire or sometimes split, very prominent, continuous with margins of sheath
Collar	narrow, divided, sometimes indistinct, yellowish green or brownish, a noticeable swelling occurring at each end of collar
Auricles	absent
Where found	throughout area in moist places; an important grass of moist meadows in the foothills of the Rocky Mountains, and northward beyond Peace River

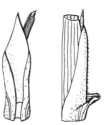

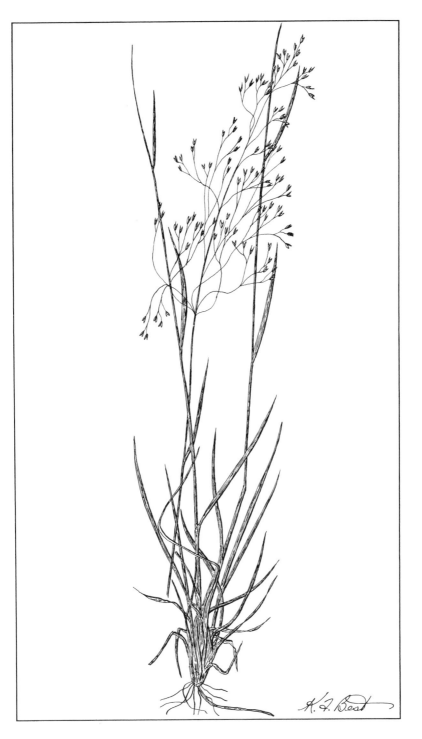

DISTICHLIS STRICTA (Torr.) Rydb.

desert salt grass, alkali grass, salt grass

Growth habit	sod-forming, perennial, with extensive scaly rhizomes
Blade	to 4 mm wide, 1 to 15 cm long, acuminate, flat to involute, ridged, scabrous on upper surface with a few long hairs especially near base, smooth below; margins very scabrous; lower blades much shorter than upper ones; folded at emergence
Sheath	round, split, usually glabrous, basal ones usually yellowish; margins overlapping, scarious
Ligule	a fringe of hairs to 0.5 mm long; fused at the base
Collar	narrow, continuous, distinct, yellowish, with tufts of long hairs at ends
Auricles	absent
Where found	throughout area; common in saline or alkaline areas, occasionally on dry slopes

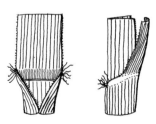

109

ECHINOCHLOA CRUSGALLI (L.) Beauv.

barnyard grass

Growth habit	annual, tufted, with fibrous roots
Blade	to 15 mm wide, 10 to 30 cm long, flat or V-shaped, glabrous, pale or yellowish green, keeled below; margins smooth or scabrous; rolled at emergence
Sheath	compressed, keeled, split, smooth, glabrous, pale green; margins hyaline
Ligule	absent
Collar	broad, continuous, glabrous, yellowish green
Auricles	absent
Where found	in gardens and waste places
Remarks	a weed in wheat fields and gardens

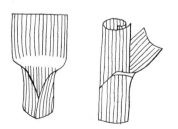

K. A. Best

ELYMUS ANGUSTUS Trin.

Altai wild rye

Growth habit	tufted, perennial, with fibrous roots
Blade	to 15 mm wide, 5 to 40 cm long, stiff, flat, acuminate, prominently veined; retrorsely scabrous on upper surface, smooth below; stomata appearing as white lines on under surface; margins retrorsely scabrous; rolled at emergence
Sheath	split, prominently veined, glabrous; margins hyaline
Ligule	to 2 mm long, membranous, acute, lacerate, ciliate
Collar	broad, continuous, yellowish, glabrous, constricted
Auricles	to 3 mm long, prominent, clawlike, clasping, hyaline
Where found	in hay and pasture fields
Remarks	introduced from Mongolia; a very coarse grass that is eaten readily by cattle in the late summer and autumn

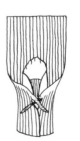

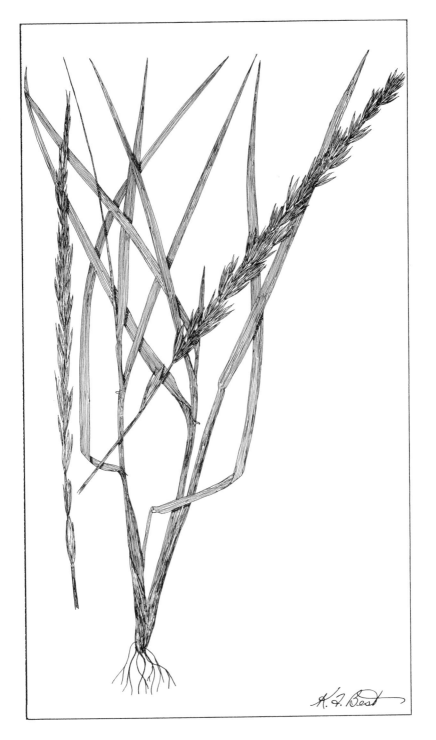

113

ELYMUS CANADENSIS L.

Canada wild rye, nodding wild rye

Growth habit	tall, erect, perennial, with short rhizomes
Blade	to 20 mm wide, 5 to 40 cm long, flat to convolute, acuminate, prominently veined above and below, dark green, sometimes glaucous; upper surface dull and slightly scabrous, lower surface glabrous with prominent midrib; margins scabrous; rolled at emergence
Sheath	round, split, prominently veined, green or glaucous, base often purplish; margins overlapping, scarious, the inner usually broadly hyaline, the outer often ciliate
Ligule	to 2 mm long, coarse-membranous, obtuse or truncate, lacerate and short-ciliate
Collar	broad, continuous, often oblique, glabrous, yellowish or light green
Auricles	to 2 mm long, clawlike, clasping
Where found	throughout area; in sand hills, along stream banks and in woods
Remarks	makes poor bedding; seldom eaten by livestock

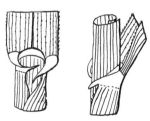

ELYMUS CONDENSATUS Presl

giant wild rye

Growth habit	very tall, tufted, perennial, with short thick knotted rhizomes
Blade	to 15 mm wide, 15 to 50 cm long, flat to convolute, acuminate, prominently veined and scabrous above, scaberulous and less distinctly veined below, fairly thick and stiff; margins scarious and often scabrous; rolled at emergence
Sheath	round, split, prominently but finely veined, smooth or scaberulous, light green, base brownish or faintly purple; margins scarious
Ligule	to 7 mm long, membranous, obtuse or truncate, lacerate
Collar	narrow, continuous, yellow, sometimes divided and indistinct, glabrous
Auricles	to 4 mm long, clawlike, clasping
Where found	along riverbanks, ravines, and moist slopes; uncommon; occasionally seeded
Remarks	single plants to 6 feet tall, and often over 1 foot wide at the base

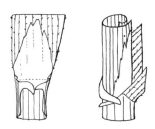

K. J. Best

ELYMUS GLAUCUS Buckl.

blue wild rye

Growth habit	tall, tufted, perennial, with fibrous roots
Blade	to 15 mm wide, 5 to 30 cm long, flat, becoming convolute on drying, usually lax, tapering but lower blades not sharp-pointed, scabrous on both surfaces, not prominently veined; margins scarious and scabrous; rolled at emergence
Sheath	round, split, smooth or scabrous, distinctly veined; margins overlapping, scarious
Ligule	to 2 mm long, membranous, truncate, lacerate
Collar	narrow, continuous or sometimes divided, glabrous, yellowish or brownish, coriaceous at the margins, often oblique
Auricles	to 4 mm long, clawlike, clasping, sometimes absent
Where found	throughout area in moderately moist, open woods and meadows; not common

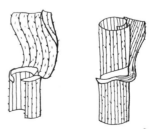

ELYMUS INNOVATUS Beal

hairy wild rye

Growth habit	tall, erect, perennial, with slender scaly rhizomes
Blade	to 12 mm wide, 5 to 25 cm long, flat to convolute, somewhat rigid, acuminate, scabrous above and below; margins very scabrous; veins more prominent above than below; rolled at emergence
Sheath	round, split, lower sheaths scabrous, upper sheaths usually smooth, prominently veined; margins scarious
Ligule	to 0.5 mm long, membranous, truncate
Collar	indistinct, narrow, divided, light green
Auricles	to 2 mm long, clawlike
Where found	throughout area in open woods and clearings; rare in the south but often abundant in the north
Remarks	seldom eaten by cattle

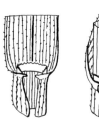

ELYMUS JUNCEUS Fisch.

Russian wild rye

Growth habit	deep-rooted, tufted, perennial, with fibrous roots
Blade	to 5 mm wide, 5 to 25 cm long, flat to convolute, acuminate, erect, somewhat scabrous on both surfaces, prominently veined; margins scabrous; rolled at emergence
Sheath	round, split, prominently veined and smooth; margins overlapping, hyaline
Ligule	to 1 mm long, membranous, obtuse to truncate, lacerate, ciliate
Collar	broad, continuous, glabrous, yellowish or light green
Auricles	to 2 mm long, clawlike, clasping
Where found	seeded for pasture in the prairie area of Western Canada
Remarks	introduced from Siberia; becoming the most common seeded grass in the southern prairies; slow to establish but very persistent

 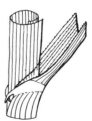

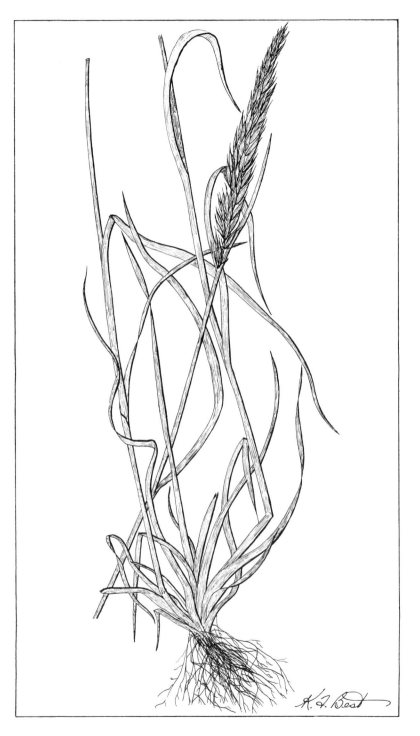

ELYMUS VIRGINICUS L.

Virginia wild rye, lyme grass

Growth habit	tall, loosely tufted, perennial, with fibrous roots
Blade	to 12 mm wide, 10 to 30 cm long, flat, acuminate, scabrous on both surfaces, distinctly nerved, somewhat keeled below; margins scabrous; rolled at emergence
Sheath	round, split, smooth, scabrous or sparsely retrorsely pubescent, light green, sometimes purplish at the base; margins overlapping, hyaline, the outer ciliate
Ligule	0.5 mm long, thick-membranous, greenish or brown-tinged, truncate, wavy, ciliolate
Collar	broad, continuous, glabrous, yellowish, often oblique
Auricles	to 1.5 mm long, clawlike, sharp, occasionally absent
Where found	throughout area in woods, clearings, and moist meadows
Remarks	this species may be distinguished from *Elymus canadensis* by its narrower blades, shorter ligule, and more scabrous blade surfaces

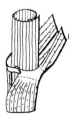

FESTUCA ELATIOR L. var. *PRATENSIS* A. Gray

meadow fescue

Growth habit	tufted, perennial, with rhizomes
Blade	to 8 mm wide, 10 to 50 cm long, bright green; upper surface dull, scabrous, and prominently veined, lower surface glossy, smooth, slightly keeled; margins scabrous; rolled at emergence
Sheath	oval, glabrous, pale green, reddish to purple at base, split to near base; margins overlapping, hyaline
Ligule	to 0.5 mm long, membranous, greenish, truncate to obtuse, entire
Collar	broad, distinct, glabrous, yellow green to cream-colored, divided by midrib; margins thin, dilated, often flexuous
Auricles	to 1.5 mm long, present, soft, clawlike or blunt, yellow green to creamy white
Where found	occasionally in cultivated hay meadows and pastures in Manitoba and western Alberta; not common
Remarks	introduced from Europe in seed mixtures; reed or tall fescue, *Festuca elatior* L. var. *arundinacea* (Schreb.) Wimm., is coarser and has scabrous leaves; it is sown in wetter places than meadow fescue

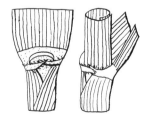

127

FESTUCA IDAHOENSIS Elmer

bluebunch fescue

Growth habit	erect, densely tufted, perennial, with fibrous roots
Blade	to 2 mm wide, 5 to 25 cm long, folded, filiform, scabrous, bluish green; veins indistinct; blades so erect as to appear continuous with sheath; folded at emergence
Sheath	flattened, keeled, split only partway, smooth or scaberulous, basal sheaths pinkish
Ligule	to 1 mm, truncate, ciliate
Collar	indistinct
Auricles	absent
Where found	Cypress Hills and southern foothills of Rocky Mountains; not common but locally abundant

FESTUCA OCTOFLORA Walt.

six-weeks fescue

Growth habit	low, erect, tufted, annual, with fibrous roots
Blade	to 2 mm wide, 2 to 10 cm long, filiform, twisted, prominently ridged and usually scaberulous below, dark green; folded at emergence
Sheath	flattened, keeled, ridged, usually retrorsely scabrous or minutely pubescent, split; margins overlapping, scarious
Ligule	to 1 mm long, membranous, truncate, ciliate, lacerate
Collar	continuous, narrow, distinct, glabrous, light green
Auricles	absent
Where found	throughout area on moist open ground, and in waste places; not common

FESTUCA OVINA L.

sheep fescue

Growth habit	densely tufted, perennial, with fibrous roots
Blade	to 1 mm wide, 5 to 15 cm long, filiform, permanently folded, bluish green, glaucous, ridged; scabrous on inner surface, usually scabrous on outer surface; margins smooth; folded at emergence
Sheath	round or slightly compressed, split, glabrous or finely pubescent, bluish green, glaucous; margins overlapping, broad, hyaline
Ligule	membranous, truncate, very short or rudimentary, ciliate
Collar	indistinct, narrow, glabrous, yellowish
Auricles	absent
Where found	throughout area in moist prairie on various soil types
Remarks	*F. ovina* is naturalized from Eurasia; the native form is *F. ovina* L. var. *saximontana* (Rydb.) Gleason; the variety is distinguished from the species by floral characters

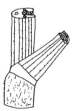

FESTUCA RUBRA L.

red fescue

Growth habit	tufted, erect, perennial, with short rhizomes
Blade	to 3 mm wide, 5 to 15 cm long, thick, V-shaped to closely folded, dark green; deeply ridged on upper surface, smooth and slightly shiny on lower surface; margins smooth; folded at emergence
Sheath	round or oval, finely pubescent, split partway only; dead basal sheaths reddish brown, often chartaceous
Ligule	to 0.5 mm long, membranous, truncate, entire or ciliate
Collar	indistinct, narrow, continuous, glabrous, pale green
Auricles	absent, or present as rounded extensions of ends of collar
Where found	in the foothills of the Rocky Mountains and northern Alberta as a native species
Remarks	commonly cultivated for pasture, hay, and lawns; the cultivated variety was selected from importations from the Atlas Mountains in Africa

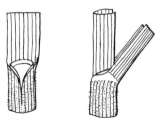

FESTUCA SCABRELLA Torr.

rough fescue

Growth habit	erect, densely tufted, perennial, often with short rhizomes
Blade	to 4 mm wide, to 50 cm long, acuminate, permanently folded; ridged and scabrous on the inner surface, scabrous on outer surface; margins scabrous; folded at emergence
Sheath	round or slightly compressed, split, smooth or scabrous; margins hyaline
Ligule	to 1 mm long, membranous, truncate, lacerate, ciliate
Collar	narrow, indistinct, glabrous, yellowish green
Auricles	absent
Where found	throughout area; common in the Wood Mountain, the Cypress Hills, the foothills of the Rocky Mountains, and the Parklands; occasionally on north-facing slopes in the plains
Remarks	single plants are often 1 foot or more across when protected from grazing

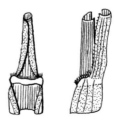

GLYCERIA GRANDIS S. Wats.

tall manna grass

Growth habit	tall, stout, glabrous, perennial, with rhizomes
Blade	to 15 mm wide, 10 to 40 cm long, flat or V-shaped, tapering to a boat-shaped tip, glabrous above and below, slightly scabrous on margins, prominently but finely veined below, with white midvein; muriform; folded at emergence
Sheath	compressed and keeled, closed to near top, but rupturing easily; smooth or slightly scabrous, pale or yellowish green, strongly striate and crossveined
Ligule	to 4 mm long, membranous, truncate to abruptly acuminate, entire or slightly undulate
Collar	conspicuous, divided, pale green or yellowish brown
Auricles	absent
Where found	throughout area in sloughs, along streams, and in wet meadows
Remarks	plants are yellowish green, coarse, with rather firm leaves having crossveins on both blade and sheath; seeds are small and very hard

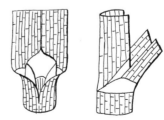

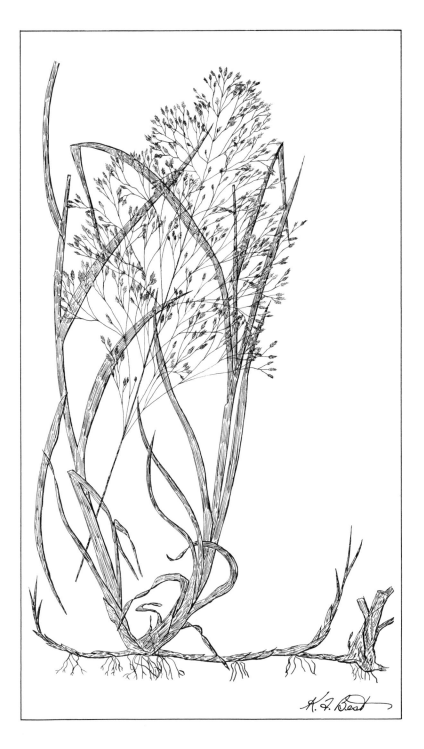

139

GLYCERIA STRIATA (Lam.) Hitchc.

fowl manna grass

Growth habit	erect, loosely tufted, perennial, with short rhizomes
Blade	to 6 mm wide, 6 to 30 cm long, flat or V-shaped, tapering to a sharp boat-shaped tip, pale green, glabrous above and below, scabrous on margins, thin, soft, crossveined; folded at emergence
Sheath	slightly flattened, somewhat keeled, closed to near top, smooth or slightly scabrous, pale green or purplish-tinged at base, finely nerved and crossveined
Ligule	to 5 mm long, membranous, obtuse, entire or lacerate
Collar	divided or continuous, indistinct, pale green, glabrous
Auricles	absent
Where found	throughout area in sloughs, along streams, and in wet meadows
Remarks	this species is distinguished from *G. grandis* by its narrower leaves, purplish-tinged sheaths, and less conspicuous crossveins on blades

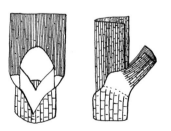

HELICTOTRICHON HOOKERI (Scribn.) Henr.

Hooker's oat grass

Growth habit	erect, densely tufted, smooth-leaved, perennial, with fibrous roots
Blade	to 5 mm wide, 2 to 12 cm long, flat to folded, firm, very erect, linear and boat-shaped at the tip, smooth; midrib prominent and thickened; margins scabrous, whitish; folded at emergence
Sheath	compressed, keeled, split, prominently veined, glabrous, rather short, pale green at base; margins hyaline
Ligule	to 5 mm long, membranous, obtuse or acute
Collar	divided, often inconspicuous, yellowish, light brown, or purplish
Auricles	absent
Where found	throughout area in places of moderate moisture; seldom abundant

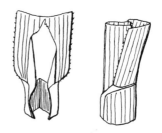

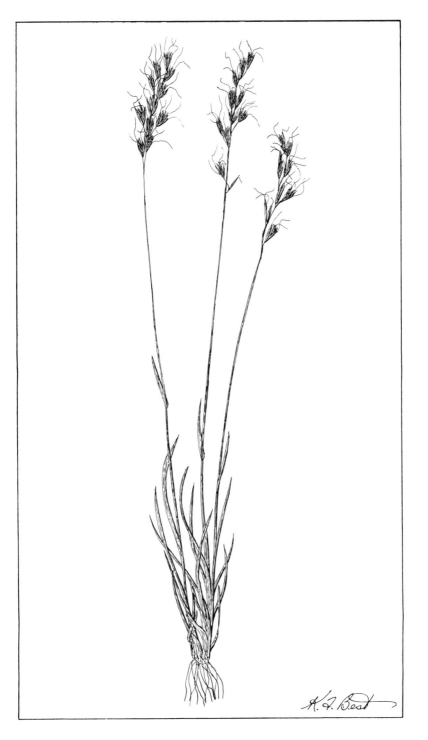

HIEROCHLOE ODORATA (L.) Beauv.

sweet grass

Growth habit	erect, sweet-smelling, sod-forming, perennial, with extensive rhizomes
Blade	to 8 mm wide, 2 to 20 cm long, flat to convolute, tapering to an obtuse point, scabrous or smooth on either surface, dark green, with fine prominent nerves on both sides; midrib white below; margins scabrous; rolled at emergence
Sheath	round, split, prominently veined, smooth or slightly scabrous, young shoots purplish at base; margins scarious
Ligule	to 3 mm long, membranous, obtuse, toothed, lacerate, sometimes ciliate
Collar	narrow, divided, light green, glabrous
Auricles	absent
Where found	throughout area in moist prairie and marsh; often an early invader on abandoned land

145

HORDEUM JUBATUM L.

foxtail barley, wild barley

Growth habit	erect, densely tufted, perennial, with fibrous roots
Blade	to 6 mm wide, 5 to 15 cm long, flat or U-shaped, acuminate, twisted, prominently veined, scabrous and usually villose above, densely puberulent or scabrous below, rarely smooth, bluish green, often purplish; margins scabrous; rolled at emergence
Sheath	round, split, distinctly veined, glaucous, pubescent, often purplish; margins overlapping, hyaline
Ligule	to 1 mm long, membranous, obtuse or truncate, lacerate, finely ciliate
Collar	medium broad, continuous, glabrous, pale green, often purplish, sometimes oblique
Auricles	absent or rudimentary
Where found	throughout area in waste places; around sloughs and marshes, and along streams; tolerates moderate alkalinity and flooding

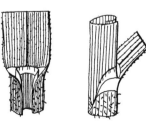

147

KOELERIA CRISTATA (L.) Pers.

June grass

Growth habit	low, erect, tufted, perennial, with fibrous roots
Blade	to 4 mm wide, 5 to 12 cm long, tapering to an obtuse tip, flat to involute, bluish green, stiff, ridged and scabrous above, keeled and usually smooth underneath, sometimes glabrous or pubescent on both surfaces; margins narrowly scarious and scabrous; folded at emergence
Sheath	round, split, scabrous and often pubescent, distinctly veined, pale green; margins scarious
Ligule	to 1 mm long, membranous, truncate to obtuse, often split, usually ciliate
Collar	medium broad, continuous or divided, yellowish green, smooth or hairy on margins
Auricles	absent
Where found	throughout area; one of the most common and widespread species, but rarely abundant
Remarks	has different growth forms in different environments, with short basal leaves in dry prairie but with few basal leaves and a taller growth where more moisture is available

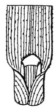

LOLIUM PERENNE L.

perennial rye grass

Growth habit	tufted, perennial, with fibrous roots
Blade	to 6 mm wide, 5 to 15 cm long, acuminate, keeled, prominently ridged on upper surface, smooth and glossy on lower surface, bright green; margins slightly scabrous; folded at emergence
Sheath	usually compressed but sometimes almost cylindrical, not keeled, glabrous, pale green, reddish at base, closed or split
Ligule	to 2 mm long, thin-membranous, obtuse, toothed near apex
Collar	narrow, distinct, glabrous, yellowish to whitish green
Auricles	small, soft, clawlike
Where found	seeded in short-term pasture and hayland, and in lawn-grass mixtures
Remarks	this introduced species resembles *Festuca elatior* except that it has leaves folded at emergence; a common pasture grass in western Europe, New Zealand, and northeastern United States

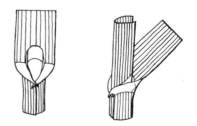

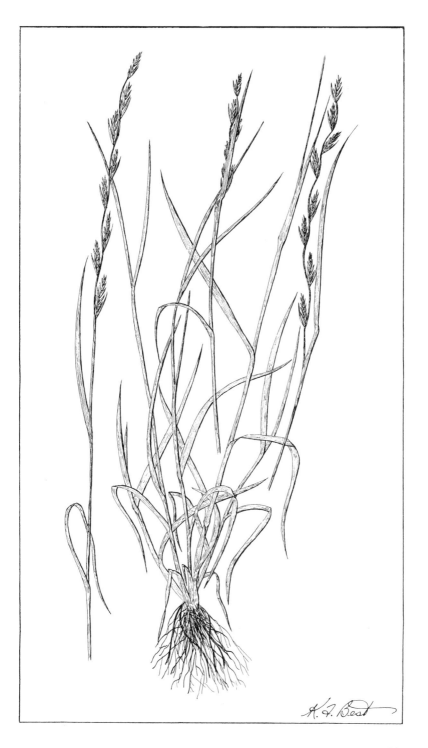

LOLIUM PERSICUM Boiss. & Hohen.

Persian darnel

Growth habit	erect, annual, with fibrous roots
Blade	to 6 mm wide, 5 to 15 cm long, flat to convolute, acuminate, twisted, ridged and scabrous above, distinctly veined and smooth or slightly scabrous below; margins slightly scabrous; rolled at emergence
Sheath	round or slightly flattened, split, prominently veined, keeled, glabrous; margins overlapping, hyaline
Ligule	to 1 mm long, membranous, brownish, truncate to rounded, lacerate
Collar	often indistinct, divided, sometimes oblique, yellowish or brown
Auricles	usually absent, occasionally rudimentary
Where found	in grain fields, gardens, and waste places
Remarks	introduced; a troublesome weed in grain fields; it will compete with wheat to a point where no grain will be harvested

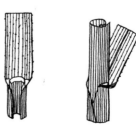

MUHLENBERGIA ASPERIFOLIA (Nees & Mey.) Parodi

scratch grass

Growth habit	low, erect, perennial, with slender scaly elongated rhizomes
Blade	to 2 mm wide, 2 to 5 cm long, flat, upper surface very scabrous; lower surface smooth, midrib prominent; margins scabrous; folded at emergence
Sheath	flattened, keeled, split, glabrous, medium green, prominently veined; margins hyaline
Ligule	to 1 mm long, membranous, lacerate, truncate
Collar	distinct, glabrous, divided by prominent midvein partway down the sheath
Auricles	absent
Where found	throughout area in moist prairie and meadows; moderately alkali-tolerant; not common

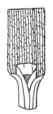 

K. A. Best 67

MUHLENBERGIA CUSPIDATA (Torr.) Rydb.

prairie muhly

Growth habit	erect, densely tufted, perennial, with hard, bulblike scaly bases, with fibrous roots
Blade	to 3 mm wide, 3 to 10 cm long, flat to folded, acuminate, prominently veined and finely rough hairy above, glabrous with prominent midvein below; margins scabrous and scarious; folded at emergence
Sheath	slightly flattened, very short, split, glabrous or slightly puberulent; margins overlapping
Ligule	to 1 mm long, membranous, truncate or rounded, lacerate, ciliate
Collar	broad, continuous, light yellow, glabrous
Auricles	absent
Where found	throughout area on very dry prairie, becoming rare towards the Parklands; often abundant on eroded calcareous slopes

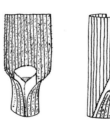

MUHLENBERGIA RACEMOSA (Michx.) B.S.P.

marsh muhly

Growth habit	erect, perennial, with stout scaly rhizomes
Blade	to 6 mm wide, 5 to 15 cm long, flat to folded, abruptly acuminate, dark green, scabrous on both surfaces; veins not prominent, midvein prominent below; margins scarious and scabrous; folded at emergence
Sheath	flattened, keeled, split, distinctly veined, smooth or scabrous; margins hyaline
Ligule	to 1 mm long, membranous, truncate to rounded, lacerate
Collar	continuous, narrow, yellowish or brownish green, glabrous
Auricles	absent
Where found	throughout area in moist meadows and margins of woods
Remarks	*M. Andina* (nutt.) Hitchc. has been found in western Manitoba. It differs in having a ligule acute to 3 mm long.

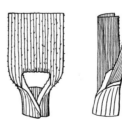

MUHLENBERGIA RICHARDSONIS (Trin.) Rydb.

mat muhly

Growth habit	low, erect, densely tufted, perennial, with extensive scaly rhizomes
Blade	to 2 mm wide, to 10 cm long, flat or involute; upper surface finely striate, slightly scabrous; lower surface smooth, midrib prominent; margins scabrous; folded at emergence
Sheath	round, split, smooth, medium green, margins hyaline
Ligule	to 3 mm long, membranous, obtuse to acute, entire, sometimes lacerate at tip
Collar	to 1 mm wide, distinct, glabrous, greenish white
Auricles	absent
Where found	throughout area on moist prairie; tolerates slight alkalinity

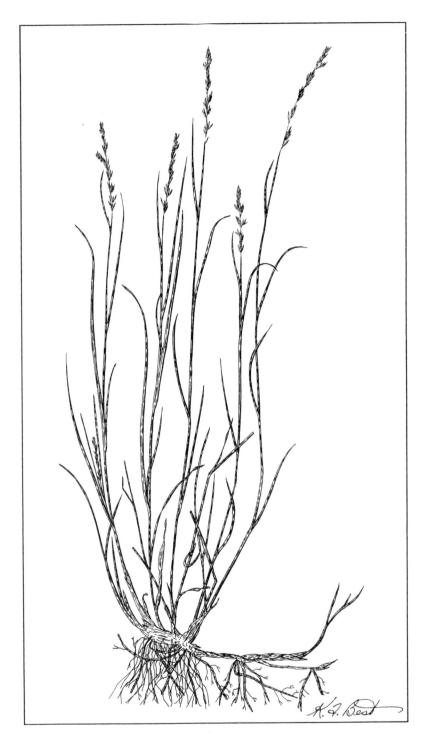

MUNROA SQUARROSA (Nutt.) Torr.

false buffalo grass

Growth habit	low, tufted, annual, prostrate, mat-forming, with fibrous roots
Blade	to 3 mm wide, 1 to 3 cm long, crowded at the nodes and ends of the branches, stiff, spreading, scabrous, flat sharp-pointed, in fascicles; rolled at emergence
Sheath	pilose at throat, often ciliate, margins loose, soon becoming papery, inflated
Ligule	to 1 mm long, a fringe of hairs
Collar	divided, narrow
Auricles	absent
Where found	extreme southern parts of area on dry prairie; rare, known from only a few locations
Remarks	introduced from the United States

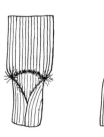

ORYZOPSIS ASPERIFOLIA Michx.

white-grained mountain rice grass

Growth habit	erect, tufted, perennial, with short rhizomes
Blade	of two types, some only 1 cm long, others to 40 cm long, all 3 to 10 mm wide, flat to convolute, erect, tapering at each end; surfaces smooth or slightly scabrous, distinctly veined above; margins very scabrous; rolled at emergence
Sheath	round, rather short, split, smooth or scaberulous, dark purple at base; margins slightly overlapping, hyaline
Ligule	to 1 mm long, membranous, ciliate, lacerate
Collar	very narrow, continuous, light green, often indistinct
Auricles	absent
Where found	throughout the Cypress Hills, the Parkland, and adjacent forest

165

ORYZOPSIS HYMENOIDES (Roem. & Schult.) Ricker

Indian rice grass

Growth habit	tall, tufted, perennial, with fibrous roots
Blade	to 5 mm wide, to 50 cm long, involute, seldom flat, long-tapering, coriaceous, coarsely ridged and scabrous above, prominently veined and smooth below; rolled at emergence
Sheath	round, split, very prominently veined, smooth or slightly scabrous; margins overlapping, hyaline, outer often fringed with hairs
Ligule	to 8 mm long, membranous, acute, often split, very conspicuous
Collar	indistinct, narrow, yellowish, often with small tufts of hairs at the margins
Auricles	absent
Where found	throughout area on sandy soils
Remarks	an important grass in sand hills, very resistant to wind action and grazing; palatable to livestock

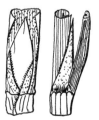

167

PANICUM CAPILLARE L.

witch grass

Growth habit	erect, tufted, annual, with fibrous roots
Blade	to 15 mm wide, 8 to 25 cm long, hispid on both surfaces, distinctly veined below, less so above, flat, acuminate, soft, keeled at base; margins scabrous, papillose-ciliate toward base; rolled at emergence
Sheath	round, split, prominently veined, dull green, often purple-tinged, conspicuously papillose-hispid; margins overlapping, hyaline
Ligule	to 2 mm long, a dense fringe of hairs fused at base
Collar	usually broad, continuous, often indistinct, yellowish green, pubescent
Auricles	absent
Where found	eastern part of area on light soils and in waste places

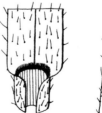

K.A. Best

PANICUM VIRGATUM L.

switch grass

Growth habit	erect, perennial, with large scaly rhizomes
Blade	to 12 mm wide, 10 to 50 cm long, flat, acuminate, constricted at base, distinctly veined, with prominent midvein, usually glabrous on both surfaces but long-pubescent on upper surface at base; margins scarious and scabrous; rolled at emergence
Sheath	round, split, with scarious and villose margins, glabrous, prominently veined, white to purplish-tinged below
Ligule	to 3 mm long, a fringe of hairs fused at the base
Collar	broad, continuous, yellowish, pubescent on margins
Auricles	absent
Where found	eastern part of area on moist prairie; rare

PHALARIS ARUNDINACEA L.

reed canary grass

Growth habit	tall, stout, erect, perennial, with long scaly pinkish rhizomes
Blade	to 15 mm wide, 10 to 30 cm long, flat, acuminate, light green, glaucous, finely veined, smooth or slightly scabrous on both surfaces, midrib prominent below; margins scabrous; rolled at emergence
Sheath	round, split, glabrous, light or yellowish green, distinctly veined, pinkish at base; margins overlapping, hyaline
Ligule	to 5 mm long, membranous, white, minutely pubescent on back, acute or obtuse, entire, lacerate or split
Collar	divided, or narrowed at midrib if continuous, glabrous, yellowish green, usually oblique
Auricles	absent
Where found	throughout area in wet places
Remarks	imported from Sweden for forage in periodically flooded areas and on irrigated soils; native forms are known

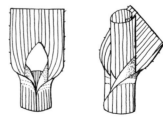

PHALARIS CANARIENSIS L.

Canary grass

Growth habit	erect, annual, with fibrous roots
Blade	to 12 mm wide, 5 to 30 cm long, flat, acuminate, twisted near apex, scabrous on both surfaces, finely nerved, midrib prominent below and extending partway down sheath; margins scarious and slightly scabrous; rolled at emergence
Sheath	round, or flattened, split, prominently veined, scabrous; margins overlapping, hyaline
Ligule	to 8 mm long, membranous, acute, lacerate
Collar	narrow, continuous, often indistinct, light or yellowish green, wider at ends than at center
Auricles	absent
Where found	in gardens and waste places, dry habitats
Remarks	introduced; grown for birdseed

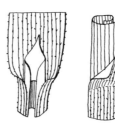

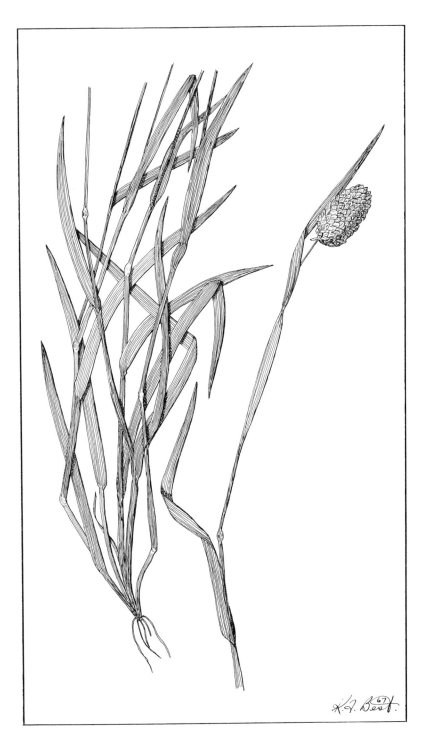

175

PHLEUM ALPINUM L.

alpine timothy

Growth habit	erect or decumbent at base, densely tufted, perennial, with a few rhizomes
Blade	to 8 mm wide, 2 to 15 cm long, flat, tapering, usually short, finely veined above, with prominent midvein below; scabrous on upper surface and margins, smooth or scaberulous below; rolled at emergence
Sheath	round, split, inflated near middle, prominently veined, glabrous, light green, often purplish at base; margins overlapping, hyaline
Ligule	to 4 mm long, membranous, truncate or obtuse, often notched on one side, rarely lacerate
Collar	narrow, often oblique, glabrous, continuous or divided, distinct, light or yellowish green
Auricles	absent
Where found	Cypress Hills, foothills of the Rocky Mountains, and Parkland; moist meadows

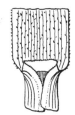

PHLEUM PRATENSE L.

timothy

Growth habit	erect, tufted, perennial, each stem growing from a bulbous or swollen base, with fibrous roots
Blade	to 12 mm wide, 5 to 25 cm long, flat, acuminate, distinctly veined, smooth or scaberulous on both surfaces, twisted, erect, light green, glaucous; scarious margins scabrous, retrorsely so at base; rolled at emergence
Sheath	round, split, distinctly veined, glabrous, light green, often purplish at base; margins overlapping, hyaline
Ligule	to 3 mm long, membranous, usually obtuse
Collar	medium broad, continuous, light or yellowish green, sometimes oblique, margins sparsely retrorse-ciliate
Auricles	absent
Where found	commonly seeded for hay and pasture in foothills and Parklands
Remarks	introduced into the United States from Europe about 1700; named for Timothy Hanson, an eighteenth-century American farmer

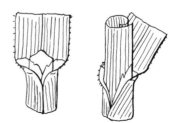

PHRAGMITES COMMUNIS Trin.

common reed, cane grass

Growth habit	very stout, erect, perennial, with stout creeping rhizomes
Blade	to 30 mm wide, 15 to 40 cm long, acuminate, narrowed at base, glabrous above and below; margins scarious and scabrous; veins fine, not very prominent; rolled at emergence
Sheath	round, split, margins scarious, glabrous, not prominently veined, light yellowish green, purplish at base
Ligule	to 1 mm long, a fringe of hairs, thick, brown, truncate, lacerate, long ciliate, pubescent on back
Collar	broad, continuous, glabrous, yellowish and usually brown on the margins
Auricles	absent or rudimentary
Where found	throughout area in wet places; fairly common in Qu'Appelle Valley
Remarks	the tallest of our native grasses, growing to 10 feet

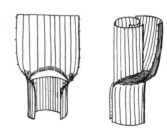

POA ANNUA L.

annual blue grass, low spear grass, annual meadow grass

Growth habit	low-growing, tufted, annual, with fibrous roots
Blade	to 4 mm wide, 2 to 8 cm long, flat or V-shaped at base, with boat-shaped tip, light green, not glossy, thin, soft, often crosswrinkled; having two distinct light lines along midvein; margins glabrous, slightly scabrous toward tip; blades widely spreading from axis of shoot; folded at emergence
Sheath	compressed and slightly keeled, glabrous, light green, split partway only; margins usually overlapping, membranous
Ligule	to 3.0 mm (usually 1.2 to 1.8 mm) long, membranous, white, acute, entire
Collar	distinct, glabrous, pale green, V-shaped
Auricles	absent
Where found	throughout area in waste places, gardens, lawns, barnyards, and footpaths
Remarks	its tufted growth, its soft, pale green and generally puckered blades, and its white conspicuous ligule are diagnostic; often found growing in lawns in mixtures with Kentucky blue grass

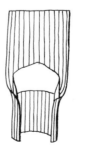
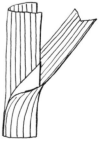

POA CANBYI (Scribn.) Piper

Canby blue grass

Growth habit	erect, tufted, perennial, with fibrous roots
Blade	to 4 mm wide, 4 to 20 cm long, flat to folded, linear, boat-shaped at tip; scabrous on upper surface with scarious margins; smooth and prominently veined below; green and glaucous; folded at emergence
Sheath	compressed, keeled above, split, scabrous, light or yellowish green at base; margins hyaline
Ligule	to 5 mm long, membranous, acute, entire
Collar	divided or continuous, pale or yellowish green, often indistinct
Auricles	absent
Where found	throughout area in moist, slightly to moderately saline meadows

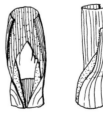

POA COMPRESSA L.

Canada blue grass

Growth habit	erect or rarely decumbent, sod-forming, perennial, with rhizomes
Blade	to 5 mm wide, 2 to 15 cm long, flat to folded, acuminate, tip boat-shaped, keeled below, broadest at base, bluish green, smooth or scabrous; veins not very prominent; margins scarious and scabrous; folded at emergence
Sheath	strongly compressed and sharply keeled, split, glabrous, green- or purplish-tinged at base; margins hyaline
Ligule	to 2 mm long, membranous, truncate or emarginate, entire, greenish
Collar	divided, narrow, glabrous, light or yellowish green
Auricles	absent
Where found	throughout area in moist meadows on poor soils; relatively abundant on sandy soils in eastern Saskatchewan and western Manitoba
Remarks	stem very flat, cannot be rolled between thumb and fingers

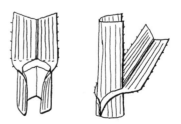

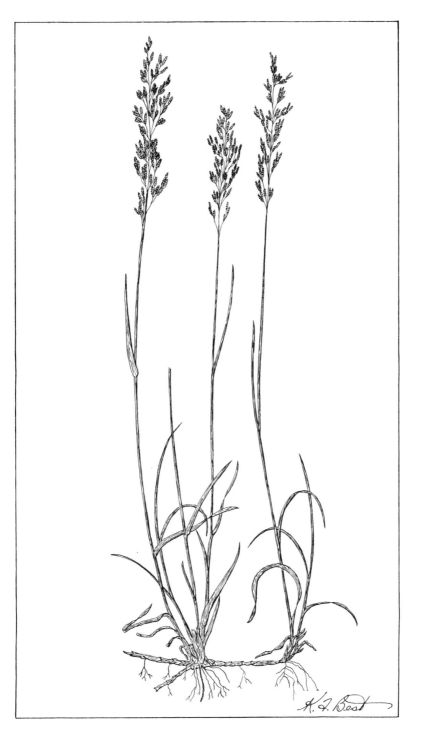

POA CUSICKII Vasey

early blue grass, Cusick blue grass

Growth habit	erect, tufted, perennial, with fibrous roots
Blade	to 3 mm wide, 5 to 15 cm long, usually folded and bristle-like, with boat-shaped tip, keeled, scabrous on margins, scabrous or smooth on surfaces; ridged on outer surface, with two prominent white veins resembling midrib, and continuing down sheath; folded at emergence
Sheath	compressed, sharply keeled, split, ridged, scabrous or smooth; margins overlapping, hyaline
Ligule	to 1 mm long, membranous, truncate, entire or slightly lacerate, very short
Collar	indistinct, very narrow, pale green
Auricles	absent
Where found	throughout area on moderately dry prairie

POA GLAUCIFOLIA Scribn. & Will.

glaucous blue grass

Growth habit	erect, loosely tufted, perennial, with few slender rhizomes
Blade	to 4 mm wide, 5 to 20 cm long, flat to folded, with boat-shaped tip, glabrous and glaucous on both surfaces, distinctly veined and prominently midribbed on lower surface; margins very scarious and scaberulous; folded at emergence
Sheath	slightly compressed, split, distinctly veined and somewhat keeled above, glabrous, often purplish at base; margins hyaline
Ligule	to 3 mm long, membranous, acute, entire
Collar	continuous or divided, light or yellowish green, often indistinct in younger shoots
Auricles	absent
Where found	throughout area in moist places but not abundant

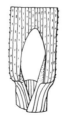

POA PALUSTRIS L.

fowl blue grass

Growth habit	tall, loosely tufted, perennial, with fibrous roots
Blade	to 4 mm wide, 7 to 15 cm long, lax, flat or V-shaped, with boat-shaped tip, broad at base; acuminate, scabrous on scarious margins and on both surfaces; midvein and two lateral veins evident on lower surface; folded at emergence
Sheath	flattened and keeled, split, distinctly veined, smooth or slightly scabrous, pale green or purplish-tinged at decumbent base; margins overlapping, hyaline
Ligule	to 4 mm long, membranous, acute, entire or lacerate
Collar	distinct, divided, pale green, glabrous
Auricles	absent
Where found	throughout area in marshy places

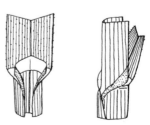

POA PRATENSIS L.

Kentucky blue grass

Growth habit	erect, perennial, with long creeping rhizomes forming a dense sod
Blade	to 5 mm wide, 5 to 40 cm long, linear with boat-shaped tip, flat to folded, keeled, distinctly veined, smooth or scabrous on both surfaces, lower one usually smooth; margins slightly scabrous; dark green; folded at emergence
Sheath	compressed but not sharply keeled, split, distinctly veined, glabrous, dark green; margins hyaline
Ligule	to 1 mm long, membranous, truncate, entire
Collar	narrow, continuous, yellowish green, sometimes indistinct
Auricles	absent
Where found	throughout area on moist prairie in fertile soils; seeded in lawns and golf courses; becomes abundant in over-grazed fescue prairie
Remarks	naturally adventive from Europe about 1700; can be distinguished from *P. compressa* by its deeper green foliage, longer and parallel-sided blades, shorter ligule, and rounder stem

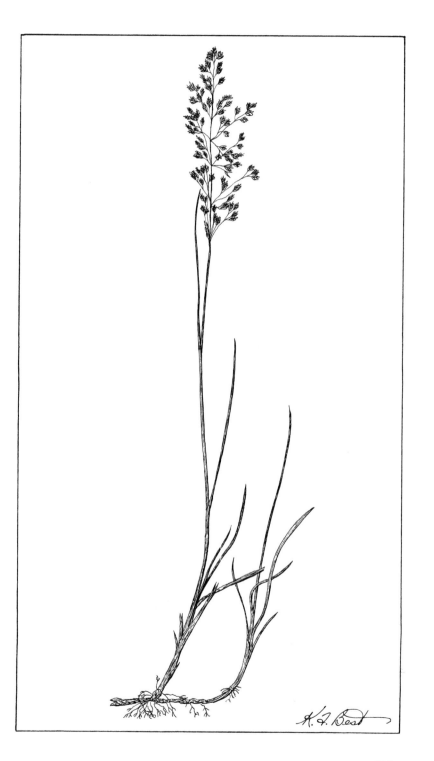

POA SECUNDA Presl

Sandberg's blue grass

Growth habit	low, erect, densely tufted, perennial, with fibrous roots
Blade	to 2 mm wide, 4 to 12 cm long, flat to folded, twisted, with boat-shaped tips, prominently veined, scabrous on both surfaces and on margins; folded at emergence
Sheath	compressed, split, smooth or slightly scabrous, prominently veined, pale or purplish at base; margins overlapping, hyaline
Ligule	to 3 mm long, membranous, acute, entire or lacerate
Collar	indistinct, divided, narrow, light green
Auricles	absent
Where found	throughout area on dry prairie
Remarks	a grass that matures its seed before July

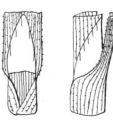

POA TRIVIALIS L.

rough blue grass, rough-stalked meadow grass

Growth habit	perennial, tufted, with stolons and fibrous roots
Blade	to 4.5 mm wide, 7 to 15 cm long, flat, acuminate, tip narrowly boat-shaped, slightly retrorsely scabrous on upper surface, glossy and keeled on lower surface; margins scabrous; bright green; folded at emergence
Sheath	compressed and sharply keeled, generally scabrous, green or purple-tinted, split only partway
Ligule	to 3 mm long, membranous, acute, entire or ciliate
Collar	broad, distinct, glabrous, divided by midrib
Auricles	absent
Where found	occasionally seeded in moist to wet pastures in eastern regions
Remarks	this grass resembles other species of *Poa* but can be distinguished by its scabrous sheath and the glossy undersurface of the blade

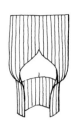 

199

PUCCINELLIA NUTTALLIANA (Schultes) Hitchc.

Nuttall's alkali grass

Growth habit	erect to spreading, tufted, perennial, with fibrous roots
Blade	to 3 mm wide, 5 to 18 cm long, flat or involute, glaucous, very scabrous above, smooth below; margins slightly scabrous; veins indistinct; rolled at emergence
Sheath	round, split, smooth; margins overlapping, scarious
Ligule	to 5 mm long, membranous, acute to obtuse, continuous with margins of sheath
Collar	to 1 mm wide, not well defined
Auricles	absent
Where found	throughout area on dry to wet saline or alkaline soils
Remarks	often growing with *Distichlis stricta*

201

SCHEDONNARDUS PANICULATUS (Nutt.) Trel.

tumble grass

Growth habit	low, tufted, perennial, with fibrous roots
Blade	to 2 mm wide, 2 to 5 cm long, usually folded, twisted and wavy, scabrous above, smooth below, scabrous on scarious margins and midrib; light bluish green; folded at emergence
Sheath	compressed, sharply keeled, split, distinctly veined, very short, usually glabrous; margins broad, hyaline
Ligule	to 3 mm long, membranous, acute, very conspicuous, and continuous with sheath margins
Collar	divided, narrow, whitish
Auricles	absent
Where found	southern part of area on open prairie, especially on abandoned land, and on sandy or other infertile soil

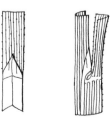

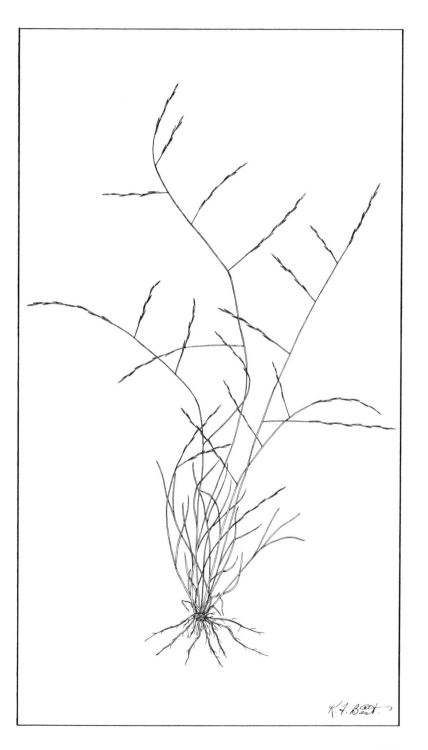

SCHIZACHNE PURPURASCENS (Torr.) Swallen

purple oat grass

Growth habit	perennial, with rhizomes, growing erect from a loosely tufted, decumbent base
Blade	to 6 mm wide, 2 to 20 cm long, flat to folded, acuminate, narrowed at base, distinctly veined, scaberulous below, smooth or scaberulous on upper surface and margins; rolled at emergence
Sheath	round or slightly flattened, closed in early stages but splitting with maturity, purplish at base, smooth or scaberulous
Ligule	to 1 mm long, membranous, truncate, lacerate
Collar	indistinct, narrow, continuous, light green
Auricles	absent
Where found	throughout area in damp woods

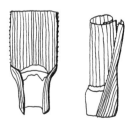

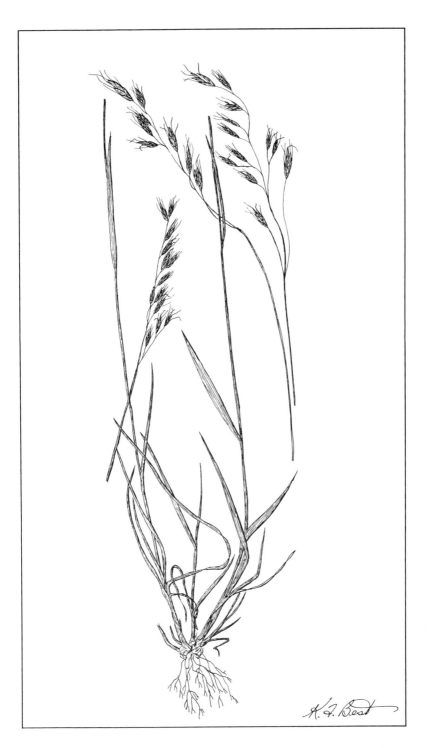

205

SCOLOCHLOA FESTUCACEA (Willd.) Link

spangletop, thatch grass, scotch grass

Growth habit	tall, erect, perennial, with stout rhizomes
Blade	to 10 mm wide, 10 to 35 cm long, flat to convolute, ridged and slightly scabrous above, glabrous and faintly nerved below, acuminate, light to yellowish green; margins narrowly scarious and scabrous; rolled at emergence
Sheath	round, split, prominently veined, glabrous, yellowish white when mature; margins overlapping, hyaline
Ligule	to 8 mm long, membranous, truncate, lacerate
Collar	divided or continuous, glabrous, yellowish or brownish green
Auricles	absent
Where found	throughout area in shallow fresh to brackish sloughs and along streams

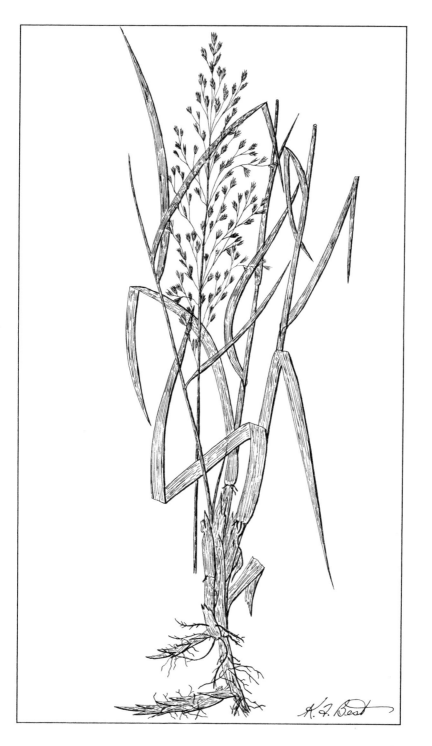

SETARIA GLAUCA (L.) Beauv.

yellow foxtail

Growth habit	erect or decumbent, annual, with fibrous roots
Blade	to 12 mm wide, 5 to 25 cm long, flat or V-shaped, acuminate, twisted, soft, drooping, glaucous, green, distinctly veined, midribbed below; slightly scabrous or smooth on both surfaces, with long twisted hairs near base on upper surface; margins smooth or scabrous; rolled at emergence from a compressed shoot
Sheath	compressed, sharply keeled, split, distinctly veined, glabrous, pale green, sometimes tinged with purple at base; margins overlapping, hyaline
Ligule	to 1 mm long, a fringe of hairs fused at the base
Collar	continuous, smooth, yellowish green, reddish or purple
Auricles	absent
Where found	in waste places, gardens, and cultivated areas; not common
Remarks	a weedy species introduced from Europe

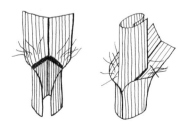

SETARIA VIRIDIS (L.) Beauv.

green foxtail

Growth habit	coarse, semierect, annual, branching at base, with fibrous roots
Blade	to 12 mm wide, 5 to 20 cm long, flat, acuminate, light green, nodding, distinctly but finely veined, with prominent midvein below; margins serrulate-scabrous; rolled at emergence from a slightly compressed shoot
Sheath	slightly compressed, split, light green or purplish at base, glabrous or appressed pubescent; margins overlapping, inner margin hyaline, outer margin ciliate
Ligule	to 2 mm long, a fringe of hairs fused at base, with longer hairs at edges of collar margins
Collar	continuous, yellowish green or red-tinged, pubescent along margins
Auricles	absent
Where found	common in waste places, gardens, and cultivated fields
Remarks	a weedy species introduced from Europe

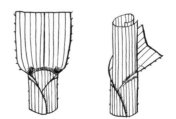

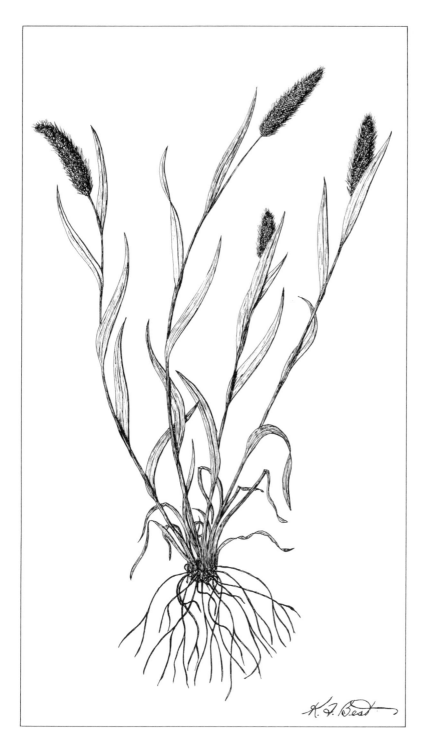

SITANION HYSTRIX (Nutt.) J. G. Smith

squirreltail

Growth habit	erect, rather short, densely tufted, perennial, with fibrous roots
Blade	to 3 mm wide, 2 to 20 cm long, flat to involute, acuminate, distinctly veined and finely pubescent on both surfaces; midvein prominent below; narrowly scarious; margins scabrous; rolled at emergence
Sheath	round, split partway down, somewhat keeled at upper end, indistinctly veined, glabrous or softly puberulent; margins hyaline
Ligule	to 1 mm long, membranous, truncate, lacerate, sometimes with wavy margins
Collar	continuous, light green, glabrous, sometimes indistinct
Auricles	clawlike when present
Where found	in very dry areas along the international boundary; rare
Remarks	may be mistaken for species of *Elymus* and *Hordeum*

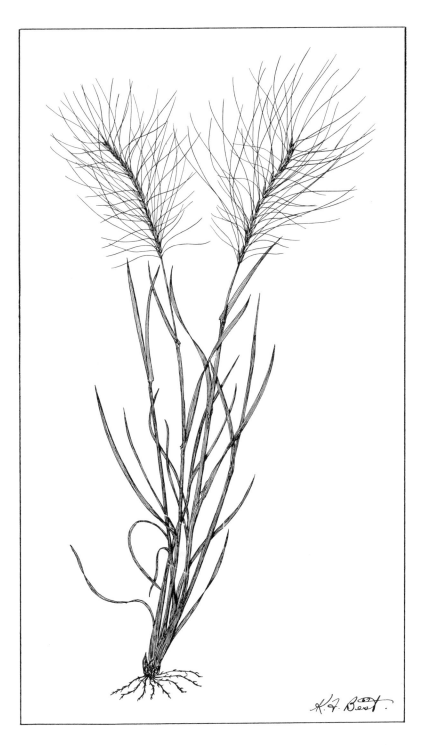

K. F. Best.

SORGHASTRUM NUTANS (L). Nash

Indian grass

Growth habit	erect, perennial, with scaly rhizomes
Blade	to 10 mm wide, 10 to 50 cm long, flat, narrowed at base, acuminate, dull green to glaucous; veins and mid-rib prominent; margins and both surfaces scabrous; rolled at emergence
Sheath	round or compressed near top, split, distinctly veined; upper sheaths usually glabrous, lower pubescent; often purplish-tinged below; margins hyaline
Ligule	to 5 mm long, membranous, obtuse to truncate, lacerate, ciliate; margins often pubescent and veined, appearing to be projections of sheath margins
Collar	continuous, glabrous, yellowish
Auricles	absent
Where found	eastern part of area on moist prairie; rare

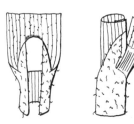

SPARTINA GRACILIS Trin.

alkali cord grass

Growth habit	tall, erect, stiff-leaved, perennial, with scaly rhizomes
Blade	to 5 mm wide, 5 to 40 cm long, flat to convolute, stiff, coriaceous, acuminate, not prominently veined; upper surface and margins very scabrous, lower surface smooth; rolled at emergence
Sheath	round, split, distinctly veined, glabrous, yellowish green or purplish at base; margins overlapping, scarious
Ligule	to 2 mm long, a dense fringe of fine hairs
Collar	divided or continuous, broad, yellowish or brownish green, glabrous
Auricles	absent
Where found	throughout area in moist, moderately saline meadows and wet places
Remarks	this grass is more common in the western part of the area; *S. pectinata* is more common eastward

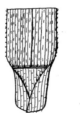

217

SPARTINA PECTINATA Link

prairie cord grass

Growth habit	tall, stout, perennial, with scaly rhizomes
Blade	to 15 mm wide, 10 to 60 cm long, flat to involute, coriaceous, long acuminate, distinctly veined above and below, very scabrous on margins and upper surface, smooth and shiny underneath, medium to light green, drooping; rolled at emergence
Sheath	round, split, distinctly veined, glabrous, pinkish at base; margins scarious
Ligule	to 4 mm long, a fringe of hairs, fused at the base
Collar	broad, continuous, glabrous, yellow or brownish green
Auricles	absent
Where found	eastern part of area, on moist prairie and in swamps; often abundant locally

SPHENOPHOLIS OBTUSATA (Michx.) Scribn.

prairie wedge grass

Growth habit	erect, tufted, perennial, with fibrous roots
Blade	to 5 mm wide, 3 to 20 cm long, flat, scabrous on both surfaces but more so on upper surface, acuminate, thin; margins very scabrous; midveins very fine below; rolled at emergence
Sheath	round, split, distinctly veined, glabrous or slightly scabrous; margins narrow, hyaline
Ligule	to 4 mm long, membranous, truncate, lacerate
Collar	narrow, continuous, or almost divided, often oblique, light or yellowish green
Auricles	absent
Where found	throughout area on moist and wet prairie; not common

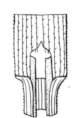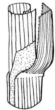

K. A. Best.

SPOROBOLUS CRYPTANDRUS (Torr.) A. Gray

sand dropseed

Growth habit	erect or decumbent, tufted, perennial, with fibrous roots
Blade	to 5 mm wide, 7 to 20 cm long, flat to involute or convolute, acuminate, distinctly veined; scabrous above and on scarious margins, smooth or scaberulous below, light green, fairly stiff; rolled at emergence
Sheath	round, split, prominently veined, glabrous, often purple-tinged at base; margins hyaline, ciliate
Ligule	to 1 mm long, a dense fringe of very fine silky hairs
Collar	broad, continuous, seldom divided, pubescent, yellow to dark green
Auricles	absent
Where found	throughout area on sandy soils
Remarks	often associated with *Calamovilfa longifolia* and *Oryzopsis hymenoides* in the sand dunes

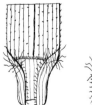

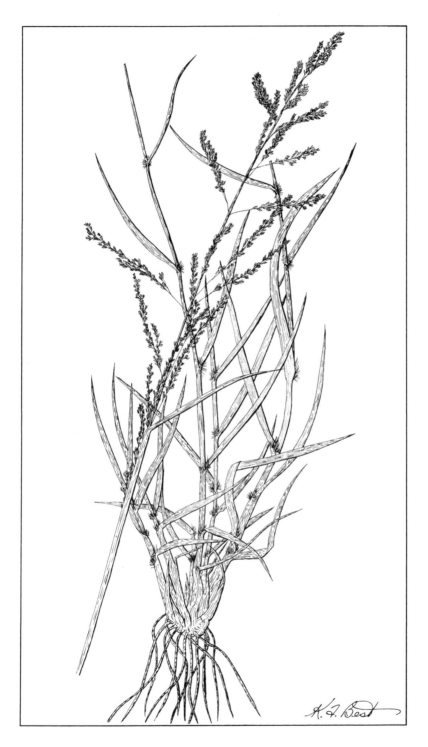

SPOROBOLUS HETEROLEPIS (A. Gray) A. Gray

prairie dropseed

Growth habit	erect, densely tufted, perennial, occasionally with short rhizomes
Blade	to 3 mm wide, 5 to 45 cm long, flat to involute, acuminate, distinctly veined, scabrous on margins and upper surface, smooth and distinctly midribbed below, light green, erect or slightly drooping; rolled at emergence from a flattened shoot
Sheath	flattened, split, distinctly veined, glabrous or pubescent, white or purplish at base; margins hyaline
Ligule	to 0.5 mm long, membranous, truncate, ciliate
Collar	continuous, medium broad, pubescent on margins, yellowish green
Auricles	absent
Where found	eastern part of area on moist prairie

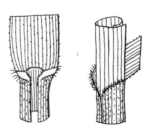

STIPA COMATA Trin. & Rupr.

needle-and-thread, common spear grass

Growth habit	erect, densely tufted, perennial, with fibrous roots
Blade	to 3 mm wide, 5 to 30 cm long, flat to involute or convolute, younger blades bristle-like, acuminate; ridged and scabrous on upper surface and margins, distinctly veined and smooth or scaberulous on lower surface; coriaceous, light green; rolled at emergence
Sheath	round or slightly compressed, split, prominently veined, glabrous; margins hyaline
Ligule	to 4 mm long, very conspicuous, membranous, obtuse or truncate, often split or frayed, continuous with sheath margins, sometimes ciliate
Collar	narrow, continuous, glabrous, light green, often oblique, usually indistinct in younger leaves
Auricles	absent
Where found	throughout area; the most common species on dry prairie

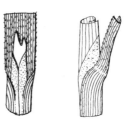

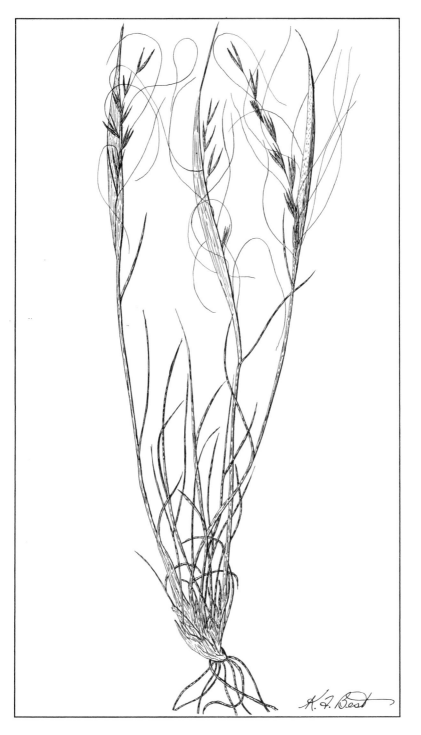

STIPA RICHARDSONII Link

Richardson's needle grass

Growth habit	erect, tufted, perennial, with fibrous roots
Blade	to 3 mm wide, 5 to 25 cm long, involute, filiform, linear, acuminate; usually scabrous on inner surface and on narrowly scarious margins, smooth or scaberulous on outer surface; light green; veins indistinct on outer surface but prominent on inner; rolled at emergence
Sheath	slightly flattened, split, distinctly veined, smooth or scabrous; margins hyaline
Ligule	to 0.5 mm long, membranous, truncate
Collar	indistinct, yellowish, continuous if evident
Auricles	absent
Where found	rare in Cypress Hills and Parklands; fairly common throughout the foothills of the Rocky Mountains
Remarks	often mistaken for *S. spartea* Trin. var. *curtiseta* Hitchc., which has an erose ligule

K. A. Best

STIPA SPARTEA Trin.

porcupine grass

Growth habit	erect, tufted, robust, perennial, with fibrous roots
Blade	to 5 mm wide, 5 to 40 cm long, flat to convolute; acuminate; ridged and scabrous on upper surface, distinctly veined and smooth on lower surface; midrib indistinct; coriaceous, light green, shiny, drooping; margins scarious; rolled at emergence
Sheath	round, split, prominently veined, white or purplish at base; margins hyaline, the outer usually ciliate
Ligule	to 5 mm long, membranous, obtuse or truncate, often split or irregular, finely ciliate
Collar	continuous, yellowish green, glabrous, often indistinct
Auricles	absent
Where found	eastern part of area on dry or moist prairie, as far west as the Qu'Appelle Valley
Remarks	a variety of this species, *S. spartea* Trin. var. *curtiseta* Hitchc., has much the same growth habit but is less robust; the ligule is about one-half as long, the notch in the center forming two lateral lobes; the variety is found throughout the area

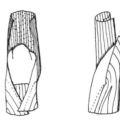

STIPA VIRIDULA Trin.

green needle grass

Growth habit	erect, tufted, perennial, with fibrous roots
Blade	to 5 mm wide, 10 to 25 cm long, flat to involute or convolute; prominently veined and scabrous on upper surface and to a lesser extent on lower surface; midrib prominent below; margins scabrous; rolled at emergence
Sheath	round, prominently veined, glabrous, split, villous near the throat; margins overlapping, scarious
Ligule	to 2 mm long, membranous, obtuse or truncate, entire
Collar	narrow, continuous, yellowish green, hairy all around but more so at margins
Auricles	absent
Where found	throughout area on moderately dry to moist, deep, fertile soils
Remarks	a variety from a plant improvement study has been named "green stipa grass," *Stipa viridula* Trin. var.

TRISETUM SPICATUM (L.) Richt.

spike trisetum

Growth habit	erect, densely tufted, perennial, with fibrous roots
Blade	to 5 mm wide, 3 to 15 cm long, flat to involute, acuminate, distinctly veined; scaberulous and puberulent above and to a lesser extent below, rarely smooth; midrib prominent below; margins scabrous and scarious; rolled at emergence
Sheath	round, split only partway down, keeled at upper end, indistinctly veined, glabrous or puberulent; margins hyaline
Ligule	to 2 mm long, membranous, obtuse, lacerate
Collar	narrow, continuous, light green, often indistinct, with few hairs at margins
Auricles	absent
Where found	foothills of the Rocky Mountains, and northern parts of area in moist meadows

235

INDEX OF COMMON NAMES OF GRASSES
IN THE SECOND SECTION

Common name	Botanical name	Page
grass		
bluebunch wheat	*Agropyron spicatum* (Pursh) Scribn. & Smith	42
brook	*Catabrosa aquatica* (L.) Beauv.	92
Canada blue	*Poa compressa* L.	186
Canary	*Phalaris canariensis* L.	174
Canby blue	*Poa canbyi* (Scribn.) Piper	184
cane	*Phragmites communis* Trin.	180
common spear	*Stipa comata* Trin. & Rupr.	226
couch	*Agropyron repens* (L.) Beauv.	38
crested wheat	*Agropyron cristatum* (L.) Gaertn.	30
Cusick blue	*Poa cusickii* Vasey	188
desert salt	*Distichlis stricta* (Torr.) Rydb.	108
desert wheat	*Agropyron desertorum* (Fisch.) Schutt.	30
dwarf oat	*Danthonia unispicata* (Thurb.) Munro ex Macoun	104
early blue	*Poa cusickii* Vasey	188
false buffalo	*Munroa squarrosa* (Nutt.) Torr.	162
flyaway	*Agrostis scabra* Willd.	50
fowl blue	*Poa palustris* L.	192
fowl manna	*Glyceria striata* (Lam.) Hitchc.	140
glaucous blue	*Poa glaucifolia* Scribn. & Will.	190
green needle	*Stipa viridula* Trin.	232
green stipa	*Stipa viridula* Trin. var.	232
hair	*Agrostis scabra* Willd.	50
Hooker's oat	*Helictotrichon hookeri* (Scribn.) Henr.	142
Indian	*Sorghastrum nutans* (L.) Nash	214
Indian rice	*Oryzopsis hymenoides* (Roem. & Schult.) Ricker	166
intermediate wheat	*Agropyron intermedium* (Host) Beauv.	36
June	*Koeleria cristata* (L.) Pers.	148
Kentucky blue	*Poa pratensis* L.	194
low spear	*Poa annua* L.	182
lyme	*Elymus virginicus* L.	124
marsh reed	*Calamagrostis canadensis* (Michx.) Beauv.	80
narrow reed	*Calamagrostis neglecta* (Ehrh.) Gaertn. Mey. & Schreb.	86
northern reed	*Calamagrostis inexpansa* A. Gray	82
northern wheat	*Agropyron dasystachyum* (Hook.) Scribn.	32
Nuttall's alkali	*Puccinellia nuttalliana* (Schultes) Hitchc.	200
one-spike oat	*Danthonia unispicata* (Thurb.) Munro ex Macoun	104
orchard	*Dactylis glomerata* L.	96
Parry oat	*Danthonia parryi* Scribn.	100
perennial rye	*Lolium perenne* L.	150
pine	*Calamagrostis rubescens* Buckl.	88
plains reed	*Calamagrostis montanensis* Scribn.	84
porcupine	*Stipa spartea* Trin.	230
poverty oat	*Danthonia spicata* (L.) Beauv. ex Roem. & Schult.	102
prairie cord	*Spartina pectinata* Link	218
prairie wedge	*Sphenopholis obtusata* (Michx.) Scribn.	220
pubescent wheat	*Agropyron trichophorum* (Link) Richt.	36
purple oat	*Schizachne purpurascens* (Torr.) Swallen	204
quack	*Agropyron repens* (L.) Beauv.	38
reed canary	*Phalaris arundinacea* L.	172

Common name	Botanical name	Page
grass		
Richardson's needle	*Stipa richardsonii* Link	228
rough blue	*Poa trivialis* L.	198
rough hair	*Agrostis scabra* Willd.	50
rough-stalked meadow	*Poa trivialis* L.	198
salt	*Distichlis stricta* (Torr.) Rydb.	108
sand reed	*Calamovilfa longifolia* (Hook.) Scribn.	90
Sandberg's blue	*Poa secunda* Presl	196
scotch	*Scolochloa festucacea* (Willd.) Link	206
scratch	*Muhlenbergia asperifolia* (Nees & Mey.) Parodi	154
slender wheat	*Agropyron trachycaulum* (Link) Malte	46
slender wood	*Cinna latifolia* (Trev.) Griseb.	94
slough	*Beckmannia syzigachne* (Steud.) Fern.	64
sweet	*Hierochloe odorata* (L.) Beauv.	144
switch	*Panicum virgatum* L.	170
tall manna	*Glyceria grandis* S. Wats.	138
tall wheat	*Agropyron elongatum* (Host) Beauv.	34
thatch	*Scolochloa festucacea* (Willd.) Link	206
tickle	*Agrostis scabra* Willd.	50
timber oat	*Danthonia intermedia* Vasey	98
tufted hair	*Deschampsia caespitosa* (L.) Beauv.	106
tumble	*Schedonnardus paniculatus* (Nutt.) Trel.	202
western rye	*Agropyron trachycaulum* (Link) Malte	46
western wheat	*Agropyron smithii* Rydb.	40
white-grained mountain rice	*Oryzopsis asperifolia* Michx.	164
wild oat	*Danthonia intermedia* Vasey	98
witch	*Panicum capillare* L.	168
muhly		
marsh	*Muhlenbergia racemosa* (Michx.) B.S.P.	158
mat	*Muhlenbergia richardsonis* (Trin.) Rydb.	160
prairie	*Muhlenbergia cuspidata* (Torr.) Rydb.	156
needle-and-thread	*Stipa comata* Trin. & Rupr.	226
redtop	*Agrostis stolonifera* L.	52
reed, common	*Phragmites communis* Trin.	180
rye		
Altai wild	*Elymus angustus* Trin.	112
blue wild	*Elymus glaucus* Buckl.	118
Canada wild	*Elymus canadensis* L.	114
giant wild	*Elymus condensatus* Presl	116
hairy wild	*Elymus innovatus* Beal	120
Macoun's wild	*Agrohordeum macounii* (Vasey) Lepage	28
nodding wild	*Elymus canadensis* L.	114
Russian wild	*Elymus junceus* Fisch.	122
tufted wild	*Agrohordeum macounii* (Vasey) Lepage	28
Virginia wild	*Elymus virginicus* L.	124
spangletop	*Scolochloa festucacea* (Willd.) Link	206
squirreltail	*Sitanion hystrix* (Nutt.) J. G. Smith	212

Common name	Botanical name	Page
three-awn, red	*Aristida longiseta* Steud.	62
timothy	*Phleum pratense* L.	178
alpine	*Phleum alpinum* L.	176
trisetum, spike	*Trisetum spicatum* (L.) Richt.	234